SEF

Esther de Waal was brought up in a country vicarage in the Welsh Borders and attended Ludlow Girls High School before reading history at Cambridge. She became Research Fellow and College Lecturer at Newnham after a period of research attached to the Department of Local History at Leicester.

After her marriage to Victor de Waal in 1960 she taught in Cambridge and Nottingham, and then joined the staff of Lincoln Theological College when her husband became Chancellor of Lincoln Cathedral. Later they moved to Canterbury, where Mrs de Waal combined her work as wife and mother of four sons with that of being mistress of the Deanery, as well as continuing her teaching work. She has been a tutor with the Open University since it began in 1971, and also taught history for the Canterbury School of Ministry. She and her husband left Canterbury in 1985.

In 1982 Mrs de Waal started 'Benedictine Experience', which brought a group of Americans to live in the cathedral precincts for ten days, to follow the Benedictine balanced life of study, worship and work.

Esther de Waal's other writings include *The Discovery of Britain, The English Tourists 1540–1840* (Routledge, 1964), *The Justice of the Peace* (Penguin, 1969), and numerous articles, amongst them 'The Benedictine Tradition and the Family' in *Journey to God, Anglican Essays on the Benedictine Way* (Malling Abbey, 1980).

Esther de Waal

SEEKING GOD

The Way of St Benedict

With Forewords by
the Archbishop of Canterbury
and
the Cardinal Archbishop of Westminster

Esther de Waal

November 1990.

Collins
FOUNT PAPERBACKS
in association with Faith Press

First published by Fount Paperbacks, London, in
association with Faith Press, in 1984
Fourth impression January 1988

© Esther de Waal 1984

Printed and bound in Great Britain by
William Collins Sons & Co. Ltd, Glasgow

The photograph of Esther de Waal on the back
cover of this book is by Bertl Gaye of Cambridge

Conditions of Sale
This book is sold subject to the condition
that it shall not, by way of trade or otherwise,
be lent, re-sold, hired out or otherwise circulated
without the publisher's prior consent in any form of
binding or cover other than that in which it is
published and without a similar condition
including this condition being imposed
on the subsequent purchaser

Dedicated in gratitude
to the cathedral community
of Canterbury

Contents

Forewords

by the Archbishop of Canterbury
and
by the Cardinal Archbishop of Westminster

Some books on the spiritual life read as if they have been composed by men of leisure for people with servants. We are right to be sceptical about the application of such writing to our own busy and distracted lives. This book is different. It was written by Esther de Waal in the midst of a very demanding professional and personal life as a wife, a teacher and a mother. It is all the better for that.

The consecrated discipline and concentration which has been needed to create this book are themselves fruits of trying to walk the way of St Benedict and they are evidence for the usefulness and realism of what is written here. 'Seeking God' is a demonstration of the profound wisdom of the Rule of St Benedict which speaks across the centuries; resonant alike for our own contemporary world as for the sixth-century monks for whom it was composed.

The 1984 Archbishop's Lent Book also shows that the Benedictine Rule not only stands the test of time but emphasizes that it has a message for all Christians irrespective of the particular church or tradition to which they belong. I am delighted that the truth of this has been underlined by the kindness of Cardinal Basil Hume, himself a Benedictine monk, in agreeing to contribute a foreword. When we give thanks for St Benedict we can all share in celebrating a saint of the Undivided Church.

Mrs de Waal calls this 'the age of beguiling paperbacks'. It is true that there is too much writing on the spiritual life which is a debilitating substitute for actual prayer and practice but this book is an exception. I have been refreshed by it and have found it personally helpful. Since Archbishops may regard themselves as experts in busy-ness and distractions, my estimate of the work may carry some weight.

I hope that this simple but profound presentation of one of the great traditions of the Christian Church will receive wide attention. It will certainly repay deep thought and meditation this Lent.

Robert Cantuar.

*

It is good to have a book on the Rule of St Benedict which comes, as the author herself says, 'from the lived experience of a housewife and mother . . .' There is a great need for books which help us to live the ideals about which we hear from the Gospel: spiritual reading is an indispensable part of our growing to know and love God more. The Rule of St Benedict has given Esther de Waal a starting point for her own reflection on the following of Christ. St Benedict's Rule, drawn in part from other ancient monastic rules, in part from his own experience, was not written for the delight of theologians and other scholars. It was written to guide his monks on how to live the Gospel in community. A family in our day can learn much from him. Many will therefore be grateful to the author of this book who has shown that ancient wisdom, when it is truly that, is also very modern and contemporary.

Basil Hume, O.S.B.

Explanation

THIS BOOK is directly inspired by Canterbury, by the cathedral and the Benedictine community which it housed in the Middle Ages. Seven years ago I had not read the Rule of St Benedict, and had only the most vague idea of what the Benedictine life involved. Like so many Anglicans, I had been aware of this country's monastic heritage in buildings and works of art. I had grown up as a child in the Shropshire parish where my father was vicar, and the church had belonged to a Benedictine priory whose ruins I saw every day from the vicarage garden. I was simply one of the many who admired abbey ruins and cathedral cloisters for what they said about past greatness. But actually to come and live in Canterbury in the context of that greatness was an entirely different experience. The house in which we lived had been the prior's lodging in monastic times; the cathedral in which we worshipped had been the church of a Benedictine community numbering among its abbots Lanfranc and Anselm; and we were surrounded by buildings which reflected the life of that community. If I walked out of the front door I passed the granary, the bakehouse and the brewhouse; if I went out by the side gate I walked through the ruins of the infirmary; the view from almost every window was of some different part of the monastery – the scriptorium, the pilgrim's hostel, and of course the great cathedral church itself overshadowing us all the time.

One day an excavation on the south side of the cathedral, in the area of the monastic graveyard, came upon two skeletons. As they lay there, anonymous, individual and yet corporate, I found myself suddenly confronted with the men whose hands had built this place and whose vision had created its way of life. That encounter led me to read the

11

Rule of St Benedict. I felt that I needed to discover something of the spirit of the Benedictine life if I was to draw strength from it and not feel crushed by what one of our sons had once called, standing under the tower of Bell Harry, 'the shadow of perfection'.

Sometimes one finds a place, a landscape, which is new and yet the forms, the shapes, the shadows seem already familiar. So it was for me with the Rule. It was neither remote nor past nor cerebral, but immediate and relevant, speaking of things that I already half knew or was struggling to make sense of. It tackled with honesty questions of personal relationships and authority and freedom; it recognized the need for stability and the need for change; it established a pattern for a balanced life; its sense of respect and reverence for people and for material things touched me immediately. I valued its insight on such day-to-day matters as hospitality or the attitude towards material possessions. Above all it spoke of a life that was essentially unheroic, much in fact like the life of any ordinary Christian family.

Although I had been thinking about this for a number of years the actual writing of this book has been done in the short space of six months. It has therefore had to take its place in a pattern of life dictated by the demands of the family, by cooking and housework, by Open University tutoring as well as the endless hospitality that we experience in a Canterbury summer when the tradition of pilgrimage still brings great numbers of visitors. This is the life of continuous interruption that I speak of in chapter VI, and often the book has been written at times of constant demands when the one reality to which I held was that promise of the Rule 'Never to despair of God's mercy'. So this is not the work of an academic or a theologian. It comes from the lived-out experience of a wife and mother with many commitments, and it springs from a conviction that the Rule speaks to those who like myself are seeking God in the midst of a busy, often confusing and exhausting daily life. I have one hope in writing this book and that is that it may serve as a first step to an encounter with the Benedictine way, for reading about it is no substitute for living it. The Rule is ancient wisdom and yet it is new, as new as the Gospel, for it is towards Christ himself that St Benedict would continually point us. It has in the past fifteen hundred years been the way by which countless Christians living under the vows in a monastic community have found God, but it speaks as well to all those of us struggling to follow our baptismal promises in the world.

Many people and many places have helped me to write this book. It would never have been possible without the support and critical encouragement of my family. I have tried to make due acknowledgement in the notes to the many Benedictine scholars whose works I have read, and if I have failed to mention any I hope I shall be forgiven. My deepest debt is to the communities of St Mary's West Malling and Bec Hellouin in Normandy, with whom Canterbury has been linked for so many centuries, though there are many others, both in England and abroad, from whom I have gained insight into the Benedictine life. But in the last resort this book is a very personal attempt to show how the Rule of St Benedict has been an inspiration and a guide to an ordinary lay Christian.

Canterbury   Esther de Waal
25th September 1983

I

St Benedict

'Let Christ be the chain that binds you'

THE WORLD into which St Benedict was born was a troubled, torn apart, uncertain world. It knew little of safety or of security, and the church was almost as troubled as the secular powers. It was a world without landmarks. It had this in common with the twentieth century: life was an urgent struggle to make sense of what was happening. The fall of Rome in A.D. 410, seventy years before the birth of St Benedict, had been a traumatic shock to the entire civilized world, and since then the invasions of successive barbarian hordes had begun to dismember the empire. By the middle of the century Huns were ravaging northern Italy and Rome had been sacked for a second time. The church too was torn apart, not only suffering through wars and political disorders but split theologically, particularly on the question of grace, which was a major concern in the fifth century. Christians must have looked back with nostalgia to the age of the Fathers and asked themselves if ever again the church could produce a St Augustine and a *City of God* to hold out the promise of peace and order and light on a scene which seemed instead to be rapidly descending into chaos. And then on this scene there appeared the man who built an ark to survive the rising storm, an ark not made with hands, into which by two and two human and eternal values might enter, to be kept until the water assuaged, an ark moreover which lasted not only for one troubled century but for fifteen, and which has still the capacity to bring many safe to land.

The builder of that ark is essentially known to us through his handiwork, the Rule. Unlike so many of the great names of Christendom, St Benedict remains curiously faceless. Our main authority for his life is the second book of the *Dialogues of St Gregory the Great*, written in Rome in 593–4, less than fifty years after his death. This life is not a biography in any modern sense of the term, for St Gregory is primarily interested in the power of working miracles and in the gift of prophecy which he saw in this *vir Dei*, this man of God. But he does at the same time give us genuine facts about his life, even if it is not always easy to separate these from the symbolic or the imagined, for he mentions actual places and people whose existence can be substantiated. Thus we learn that St Benedict was born around the year 480 in the Umbrian province of Nursia, into what the *Dialogues* describe as 'a family of high station'. He went to Rome to study liberal arts but then abandoned his studies and left the city, first for a stay of about two years at Affile and then for Subiaco, where for three years he lived a solitary life in a cave on a hillside, a mountain fastness surrounded by scenery formidable in its wild beauty, with a view of the ruins of Nero's palace and the broken arches of a Roman aqueduct lying below, symbols of the crumbling imperial greatness. Here he was quite alone apart from the ministrations of a neighbouring monk who brought him bread but kept his whereabouts secret. Ultimately he was discovered by such numbers of disciples that he established twelve small monasteries, scattered close by on the hillside, each with about a dozen monks. After some years, probably in 528 or 529, he left the valley and, taking some of his monks with him, he went south to Monte Cassino, the imposing mountain mass rising up in the central Apennines. After destroying a pagan shrine he built his new monastery in its place, and here he remained for the rest of his life. Once a year he met his sister St Scholastica who had established herself nearby with her community of nuns. Here he acquired a widespread reputation as a holy man, and here, sometime in the middle of the sixth century, he died, on a date which is traditionally held to be 21st March 547. His remains were not, however, destined to be allowed to lie in peace. About forty years after his death the monastery was destroyed by Lombards and left abandoned until it was refounded in about 720. There is considerable uncertainty about what actually did happen, but it seems that at some time in the mid-seventh century the remains of St Benedict and St Scholastica, which had been buried in the same tomb, were removed to France and the relics of St Benedict ultimately came to the abbey of St Benoît-sur-Loire, where they remain today.

The twenty-eight chapters of the Life as St Gregory presented it in the *Dialogues* concentrate mainly on wonder working miracles and encounters with demons, much that seems difficult and unedifying to the modern reader. But to dismiss this too quickly would be to lose the opportunity of finding here another dimension to our understanding of St Benedict's life. For the interest of the author does not lie in chronology and in events, it is much more in the line of biblical story telling, the plot line rooted in a journey motif. As St Gregory unfolds the life it is seen as a quest, a pilgrimage set in the narrow mountain passes and the broad sweep of plains that will ultimately lead St Benedict to the mountain top. There is something here of what the Rule itself promises, starting with a narrow gate and then widening out. Perhaps too it reflects something of what St Benedict, bred and shaped in the mountains, knew himself. But there is more to it than this. St Gregory wanted his readers to see in St Benedict an example of God at work in man's life. He illustrates the law of paradox; genuine fruitfulness comes from what at first seems sterile; life comes out of death. Again nothing touches more closely the thinking of the Rule itself, with its central theme of dying and rebirth.

Yet the St Benedict of the *Dialogues* still eludes us as a person. The Rule itself remains the source which ultimately reveals the personality of the man. For both its aim and its language set it apart from other similar monastic rules, and it is this which tells us so much about its author. The academic discussion of the degree of originality of the Rule is mercifully something which does not concern us here. An immense amount of impressive scholarship has been devoted to a question which is of the greatest significance to contemporary scholars, but which would in all probability have seemed absurd and irrelevant to St Benedict himself. He was happy to take what was good from the existing monastic heritage, to make it his own, and to colour it with his own personal experience. As he looked round he found various types of monastic life with their own traditions and achievements. There were some forms of the life which allowed much scope for individual development and for the life of solitude; others stressed more the value of a corporate life in a settled community. He drew these different strands together, and the discovery of the sources from which he derived much of his own material does not reduce the importance of his own contribution, rather it enhances it in showing his extraordinary skill in selecting and blending elements to form a balanced, positive and complete unity. But this is not just the work of an intellectual, the cerebral achievement of a skilled codifier. This is the work of a man who has lived what he is writing about, both in the cave at Subiaco and in the monastic enclosure at Monte Cassino. The consummate wisdom which it shows could only have emerged from a long and thorough assimilation, not simply in his mind but in his whole being.

It is his new understanding of the relationships between the members of the community that is the great breakthrough. The older ideal had been essentially that of the novice finding a holy man and asking to learn from him, and the monastery had been a group of individuals gathered round the feet of a sage. One of these earlier rules, the Rule of the Master, had given enormous power to the abbot. St Benedict changes this almost exclusively vertical pattern of

18

authority by emphasizing the relationships of the monks with each other. They are of course disciples who have come to the monastery to be trained, but they are also brothers bound in love to each other. So for St Benedict the monastery has become a community of love and the abbot a man who is expected not to be infallible or omniscient, but a man who will exercise his discretion as the circumstances demand. The Rule of the Master had used the word 'school' nine times, St Benedict uses it once only; as well as *magister*, master, he speaks of a loving father. The way in which the monks relate to each other is of little interest in the Rule of the Master; the Rule of St Benedict devotes three splendid chapters to it (69–71), with chapter 72 a master-piece on what is involved in loving one another.

> The monks are to bear with patience the weaknesses of others, whether of body or behaviour. Let them strive with each other in obedience to each other. Let them not follow their own good, but the good of others. Let them be charitable towards their brothers with pure affection. (72. 5–8)

Textually his Rule may be almost the same in many of its phrases as that of the Master; but in its mood and its outlook it is a world apart. This chapter above all reflects the Benedictine ideal; this is the imprint of St Benedict himself. The ark which he was building was to contain a family.

The monasteries of the sixth century, as they grew in St Benedict's lifetime, were essentially small and simple, intended for a group of about a dozen, and all the daily activity had the characteristics of a large family at work. The monastery iself would be a small single-storey building, and scattered around would lie offices, outhouses, farm-sheds. Neither dormitory, refectory or oratory needed to be large or elaborate. The cloister was a thing of the future. The small community who gathered here as a Christian family to live, work and pray together would probably make small claim for themselves, for most were simple men, few were priests or scholars. The pattern of the day was established by the *opus Dei*, the work of God, the purpose of the monastic life. So seven times a day the monks would gather in the oratory, at hours which varied slightly between the summer and the winter months, to say together those offices which began soon after midnight with Vigils, were followed at daybreak by Lauds, and continued until the day ended, last thing in the evening, with Compline. The rest of the time was fully occupied with domestic or agricultural work, with study and reading, besides two meals and the hours of sleep. Here were men living together to serve God and save their souls, glad to care for those who sought them out but content to remain essentially ignorant of the world outside their walls.

At the time of his death St Benedict's Rule was one amongst many. Within a century or two St Benedict himself had become the patriarch of western monasticism and his Rule the most influential in the Latin church. From the seventh century onwards the Benedictines brought both Christianity and civilization to much of Europe, *Cruce, libro et atro* as the tag ran, with cross, book and plough. Before long the whole of western Christendom was carrying a scattering of monasteries like a mantle. The 'monastic centuries' had begun. It now becomes possible to see how deeply the life of Christendom was to be shaped by the Benedictine presence. Whereas in the very earliest days monks had gone out into the desert leaving behind them a comparatively sophisticated life, now that pattern was reversed. In a world in which barbarian invasion, political uncertainty, and the power of the sword seemed the most immediate realities, and in a simple agrarian world where parishes were served by priests of humble peasant birth, the monasteries came to stand out as centres of light and learning. Here men and women might expect to find a rich liturgical life, informed devotion, a love of learning and intelligent companionship, in communities now much larger than those of the sixth century. The small buildings housing a dozen men became a great complex, possibly for a hundred or more monks, with a large church, accommodation for the sick and the infirm, guest houses, and offices to administer extended estates. As time went on they accumulated stores of illuminated manuscripts, relics and works of art. Pilgrims and visitors from every rank of society from crowned heads to poorest peasants, came in search of prayers or alms, protection and hospitality. This mingling of the enclosed life with the life outside the walls was certainly not something foreseen by St Benedict, but it became too deeply part of the way of life to be eradicated. It meant many different things to many people. At one level it meant that abbots often became figures of political importance; at another that the surrounding countryside learnt much about agricultural efficiency and expertise. To sketch the history of the Benedictines in the Middle Ages would be not only to write a history of the church, it would be to write a history of medieval society as well. In every country of Europe the black monks, as they became known, established themselves as landowners, administrators, bishops, writers, artists. Half the cathedrals of England were under Benedictine rule. New foundations were appearing all the time, not least those which sprang up under the stimulus of the monastic renewals which from the tenth century brought a re-ordering, a re-emphasis of the original Rule. First Cluny and then Citeaux appear as offshoots of the main trunk, each responding to the new demands of an increasingly complex society, yet without losing touch with the heart of the Rule. First the Cluniacs emphasized the good order and administration, and put magnificent worship to the fore; then the Cistercians recovered the role of austerity and of hard manual work which they felt had become neglected. By the beginning of the thirteenth century in England and Wales alone the number of houses of black monks had grown from fifty in 1066 to three hundred in 1200, and the white monks (the Cistercians were distinguished by their habits of undyed wool) by 1200 had some seventy houses. Few people in England today live far from the ruins of some great Benedictine or Cistercian foundation, or do not know cathedrals which were in the Middle Ages the churches of some Benedictine community.

But while we pay homage to the power and presence of the past we might all too easily forget the continuing link of the Church of England with the Benedictine life. For the Benedictine presence, so strong in England in the Middle Ages, left its mark on the church at the time of the Reformation. It was Cranmer's genius to condense the traditional monastic offices into the two Prayer Book offices of Matins and Evensong, and their continued usage through the following centuries has shown how highly appropriate for parish church and cathedral worship those adapted offices can be. It is hardly too much to claim that the Benedictine spirit is at the root of the Anglican way of prayer, as both clergy and laity have been nourished by the daily recitation of the psalms and the regular reading of the Scriptures. And, if the Benedictine way stands above all else for balance and moderation, so also does the Anglican *via media*.

Today many thousands of men and women, some Anglican and many more Roman Catholic, are following the monastic life according to the Rule of St Benedict. How is it possible that one common bond can link together, over a space of fifteen hundred years, those first small communities of a dozen, those great powerful medieval establishments, and the amazing variety of contemporary expressions of the same life? How is it possible that this same Rule can also speak to men and women who are trying to follow Christ without undertaking the commitment to community? Perhaps one of the stories which St Gregory tells about St Benedict may hint at the answer. It comes not from the Life but from the third book of the *Dialogues*. A certain hermit named Martin had chained himself to the side of his solitary cave near Monte Cassino. When he heard of it St Benedict sent him this message: 'If you are indeed a servant of God, do not chain yourself with chains of iron. But rather, let Christ be the chain that binds you.' St Benedict points to Christ. It is as simple as that. Christ is the beginning, the way and the end. The Rule continually points beyond itself to Christ himself, and in this it has allowed, and will continue to allow, men and women in every age to find in what it says depths and levels relevant to their needs and their understanding at any stage on their journey, provided that they are truly seeking God.

THOUGHTS AND PRAYERS

Come my children, listen to me:
and I will teach you the fear of the Lord.

(Psalm 34:11)

There was a man of holy life, Benedict by name, and the
benediction of God was upon him.

(St Gregory, Dialogues, II, I)

Love takes to itself the life of the loved one.
The greater the love, the greater the suffering of the soul.
The fuller the love, the fuller the knowledge of God.
The more ardent the love, the more fervent the prayer.
The more perfect the love, the holier the life.

(Staretz Silouan)

Holy and blessed Benedict,
the grace of heaven has made you rich
with such full blessing of goodness
not only in order to raise you to the glory you desire,
to the rest of the blessed, to a seat in heaven,
but that many others be drawn to that same blessedness,
wondering at your life,
stirred by your kind admonitions,
instructed by your gentle doctrine,
called on by your miracles.
Benedict, blessed of God,
whom God has blessed with such wide benediction,
I pour forth my prayer to you
with all the fervour possible;
and implore your help with all the desire possible;
for my need is too great; I cannot bear it.

(St Anselm)

A swimmer plunges into the water stripped of his garments to find a pearl; a monk stripped of everything goes through his life to discover in himself the pearl – Jesus Christ; and when he finds him, he seeks no longer for aught existing beside him.

(Isaac of Turin)

Miracles may show me the saint, they do not show me how he became a saint: and that is what I want to see. It is not the completed process that intrigues me: it is the process itself: for you see, my work is not to be a saint. Tell me what was churning in his soul as he battled his way up from selfishness and the allurements of sin to the great heart of God.

(M. Raymond, O.C.S.O.)

If anyone would like to get the true picture of this man of God let him go to the Rule he has written, for the holy man could not have taught anything but what he had first lived.

(St Gregory, Dialogues, II, 26)

> Almighty God,
> by whose grace St Benedict,
> kindled with the fire of your love,
> became a burning and a shining light in the church:
> inflame us with the same spirit
> of discipline and love,
> that we may walk before you
> as children of light;
> through Jesus Christ our Lord.

NOTES

The idea of describing the Rule as an ark comes from an article by the Rev. Prof. Gordon Rupp, 'St Benedict, Patron of Europe', *Church Quarterly Review*, July 1968, Vol. 1, No 1, pp. 13–21, to which I am indebted for this and for other comments in the opening sections of this chapter.

There are a number of editions of the Second Book of the *Dialogues*. I used a translation by Myra L. Uhlfelder, published by the Boob-Merrill Company Inc., New York, 1967. This interpretation of St Gregory's Life owes much to the introduction to the Collegeville text of the Rule, 'St Benedict of Nursia' pp. 73–9, and to Ambrose Wathen 'Benedict of Nursia: Patron of Europe, 480—1980', Part II, 'The Vir Dei Depicted by Gregory the Great', *Cistercian Studies*, 1980, XV, pp. 229–38.

The point on page 18 about the consummate wisdom which the Rule reflects is further discussed in a chapter by Claude J. Peifer O.S.B. 'The Rule of St Benedict – Present State of the Question', *The Continuing Quest for God*, ed. William Skudlarek O.S.B., Liturgical Press, Collegeville, 1980.

A useful article on the present state of scholarship on the Rule is Sir Richard Southern, 'St Benedict and his Rule', *Ampleforth Journal*, Summer 1982, LXXXVII.1, pp. 16–28.

In *The Making of the Benedictine Ideal*, the Thomas Verner Moore Memorial Lecture for 1980, published by St Anselm's Abbey, Washington D.C., 1981, the Rev. Prof. Owen Chadwick makes a most illuminating comparison of the Rule of the Master and the Rule of St Benedict. I made particular use of what he had to say on pages 18–19.

It is an impossible task to condense the history of the Benedictine Order in the Middle Ages into one or two paragraphs. There are endless excellent studies which will fill out the story. Two of the best short accounts are David Knowles *Christian Monasticism*, World University Library, Weidenfeld & Nicolson, 1969, and George Zarnecki *The Monastic Achievement*, Thames

& Hudson, 1972. The best book on the English Benedictines remains David Knowles *The Monastic Order in England,* 2nd ed., Cambridge, 1963.

Robert Hale's book *Canterbury and Rome: Sister Churches,* Darton Longman & Todd, 1982, devotes one chapter to a discussion of the Benedictine roots of Anglicanism, 'Discovering Consanguinity: the Monastic Benedictine Spirit of Anglicanism', and he also has much of interest to say on how much he finds in common between Benedictine balance and moderation and the Anglican *via media*.

In 'Thoughts and Prayers', the Staretz Silouan quotation comes from *The Undistorted Image,* Faith Press, 1958.

St Anselm's prayer is taken from *The Prayers and Meditations of St Anselm,* translated by Sister Benedicta Ward S.L.G., Penguin, 1973, and the extract by M. Raymond is from the introduction to *The Family that overtook Christ,* Clonmore and Reynolds, Dublin, 1944.

The final prayer is the collect of an abbot in the Alternative Service Book.

II

The Invitation

'Let us set out on this way, with the Gospel for our guide.'

'NOW IS THE HOUR for us to rise from sleep . . . let us open our eyes . . . let us hear with attentive ears . . . run while you have the light of life.' That urgent call to awake, to listen, to take action, was addressed to the sixth-century monks of Monte Cassino, the monastic community established by St Benedict in the Apennine hills of central Italy. The phrase is taken from the Rule, that brief working document which in no more than nine thousand words sets out the aims and practice of the monastic life as St Benedict presented it. It is clearly set out, divided into seventy-three chapters, which look in turn at all the essentials of worship, work, study, hospitality, authority, possessions demanded by a life lived out in community following the three Benedictine vows of obedience, stability and *conversatio morum*. Fifteen hundred years on it has lost nothing of its freshness or immediacy. It speaks to all of us. Right at the very start of that Prologue its approach is wide open: 'Whoever you may be . . . he that has ears to hear.' A variety of images comes tumbling out as in his excitement St Benedict addresses his listeners at one moment as recruits for the army, and the next as workmen in God's workshop, then as pilgrims on the road, then as disciples at school. Each of us is to hear the call in different ways; it will strike one chord in one person and another in the next. But one thing we all share in common. The message is to be heard now, we must rouse ourselves, shake ourselves out of our apathy. The Rule questions the assumptions by which we live and looks at some of the most basic questions that we must all face. How do we grow and fulfil our true selves? Where can we find healing and grow into wholeness? How do we relate to those around us? to the physical world? to God? If we think of all the alienations that we must resolve – those alienations that we find in the story of Genesis and of the fall – from one another, from the natural environment, from God himself – the alienations within ourselves remain the starting point. So the familiar words of the western world, which can be heard all the time in conferences and consultations, in sermons and discussions, are also the theme words of the Rule: roots, belonging, community, fulfilment, sharing, space, listening, silence. The sense that men and women need to love and be loved if they are to become fully human; that they need a place in which to belong, and that not merely in a geographical sense; that they need freedom and yet they must accept authority. The Rule knows much about the continuing paradox that all of us need to be both in the market-place and yet in the desert; that if we join in common worship yet we have also to be able to pray alone; that if commitment to stability is vital so also is openness to change. There is no evasion here of the complexity of life, and yet the final paradox is that running the way to God appears modest and manageable while at the same time it is total. These are the demands of extreme simplicity which cost everything.

All of us need help if we are to face up to the realities demanded of us if we are to make our way to God as whole and full people. There is nothing unfamiliar in that appeal of the Prologue, nothing new. It is ancient wisdom and yet it is contemporary. It is an appeal to the divine spark in everyone, never totally extinguished but in need of re-kindling. In an age of extreme complexity men and women look for vision even more desperately, since without vision there is no hope. That is why the Rule of St Benedict speaks to all of us – it answers a deep need.

The connotations of restriction, restraint, control, even of bureaucracy, which the word 'rule' carries with it today do not, however, encourage most of us to look very warmly on such a guide, such an approach. Even St Benedict's modest claim that it is no more than 'a little rule for beginners' does not reassure us. Yet the Rule of St Benedict is neither rule-book nor code. It does not dictate; it points a way. It is a piece of creative writing which combines a firm grasp of essentials with a confident flexibility about their practical application. For the past fifteen centuries men and women living out the Benedictine monastic life have come back to it as the spring and source of their personal renewal and their community reform, finding it still relevant, apposite, inspiring. So too those of us on the outside of the monastic enclosure, in whatever walk of life, if we let it speak to us will also find that it answers our needs with its immediate, practical, vivid wisdom.

Nowhere does St Benedict suggest that he is interested in encouraging unusual people to perform spectacular feats. His monks are ordinary people and he will lead them in ways that are accessible to ordinary people. In fact the importance of the weak and the ordinary is one of the great guiding principles of the Rule, one which 'makes it possible for ordinary folk to live lives of quite extraordinary value,' as Cardinal Basil Hume puts it. Time and again the Rule makes allowances for human weakness. 'In drawing up its regulations we hope to set down nothing harsh, nothing burdensome' (Prol. 46). The essence of the Benedictine approach is distilled in a small phrase of Thomas Merton's, written in 1945 right at the start of his monastic life in the Cistercian abbey of Gethsemani in Kentucky when he wrote of 'that concern with doing ordinary things quietly and perfectly for the glory of God which is the beauty of the pure Benedictine life.'

Perhaps on first reading much of the Rule might appear rather prosaic, with chapters on such mundane affairs as food and sleep and clothing, the duties of porter or cellarer or server. It *is* indeed mundane, of the world, and all the more important for that reason. But then on re-reading it, what had seemed rather dry becomes vibrant and vital because in exploring the Rule we find that this is a description of day-to-day living which revolves around Christ, both individually and corporately. For essentially the intention is to heighten an awareness of Christ himself, that Christ who has seen us in the crowd and called out to us, and who is at once the start of our journey and also the goal. 'Seeking his workman in a multitude of people, the Lord calls out to him and lifts up his voice again: Is there anyone here who yearns for life and desires to see good days? (Psalm 33 (34):13). If you hear this and your answer is 'I do' . . . See how the Lord in his love shows us the way of life' (Prol. 14–16, 20). And that way is essentially our own highly individualistic way. Chapter 40, which deals with a most practical matter, the measure of drink, opens with a quotation from 1 Corinthians: 'Each man has his special gift from God, one of one kind, another of another.' This really says something very important about the Rule. It is offering a basis on which each individual is to grow and develop. St Benedict was not concerned to stifle the spirit with over-legislating. He was far more interested in educating the individual to recognize the need of the moment and to respond to it appropriately than in laying down clear-cut directives for every conceivable contingency. This is of course the secret of its power. Dom David Knowles, himself a Benedictine, wrote of this with characteristic warmth and simplicity.

No one seriously coming at Christian perfection can go to the Rule for help and come away feeling that he read advice suitable only for a particular call or a particular stage of the religious life. Each finds there what he seeks. The Rule has something of the divine impersonality, without limitations and yet intensely individual, of the Gospel teaching; nor should this surprise us, for the Rule is the Gospel teaching.

31

'Let us set out on this way, with the Gospel for our guide' (Prol. 21). Right from the start, when the Prologue declares, 'the Scriptures rouse us when they say, "It is high time for us to arise from sleep"', we find that the primary concern of the Rule is to confront us as forcefully as possible with the Gospel and all its demands. The Word of God is directly addressing the reader or the listener. For St Benedict is himself a man grasped by the Word of the Lord, a man who listens himself and so calls for listening in others. If we listen we have the chance of the gift of relationship in Christ; if we fail to listen we throw away that chance. Two vivid images are used in the Prologue to describe the Word and to show the role it is to play in our lives. It is 'the light that comes from God' (9) and then 'the voice from heaven' that calls out its challenge. That challenge is a phrase from the invitatory psalm 95 (94) used each day at the office: 'If you hear his voice today do not harden your hearts' (8). It would be difficult to think of anything more urgent, more immediately rooted in the here and now of this moment in time, in today and not in tomorrow or yesterday. Here is an analogy between the daily rising from sleep to hear the words of Scripture and the taking up of the religious life in general as a rising from sleep. A light to waken and a voice to rouse: the Word must be heard, it demands response! At the very end of the Rule, in chapter 73, St Benedict picks up this point again equally firmly, in a tone of voice that brooks no excuses. It is Scripture itself which has the divine authority, which is 'the truest of guides for human life'. So in some ways the whole of the Rule might be thought of as an inclusion, a commentary, a practical working out of this central theme of the primacy of the Word. The Rule is simply an aid for us to live by the Scriptures. Almost every page of the Rule carries either a direct quotation from the Bible or reflects some biblical allusion. The New Testament is used slightly more often than the Old, and altogether there are probably well over three hundred references. It remains almost impossible to come to a certain estimate for the simple reason that even if the rule is not using a direct quotation it is so thoroughly soaked in the language and the imagery of the Bible that much of the writing has a biblical flavour, and carries a biblical resonance.

What the members of a Benedictine community sought from the Word was not knowledge but strength, whereas we in the twentieth century have reversed those priorities. This makes it easy to question whether St Benedict is not rather naïve in his use of Scripture, whether what he does with the Old Testament is justified or not. To read the Rule in such an academic way is to prevent ourselves from experiencing its full power. St Benedict's essential aim was to make Scripture a living experience for his community with all the means at his disposal. 'Holy Scripture cries aloud!' is how he opens chapter 7. We are continually confronted with God speaking. There is no escape.

When he wrote the Rule the Bible was essentially a book that was heard rather than read. Since most monasteries and convents had only a limited number of books, and since in any case most reading would take place during the saying of the offices, and even private reading would involve reading to oneself in a muted voice, comparable to reading a poem aloud quietly for full effect, Scripture became a message spoken *this* day to *this* disciple. But it was not simply the reading technique that was responsible. The 'cry' of Scripture is perceived as the voice, the call of God. When the call is heard it must be embraced as a personal message with its living demands addressed to each individual. God's word is not something static, past and dead; something lying inert between the covers of a book. It is what it is called: the manifestation of a living person whom one recognizes by the tone of voice. The call is not simply something out of a distant past; it comes today and it comes to elicit a response from us and to engage us in dialogue. In an age of beguiling paperbacks offering attractive ways to God through every conceivable means, the Rule stands firm in its relentless demand that we listen to the Word, that we never fail to remember that the Word remains our point of reference. Its aim, which the Prologue shows so clearly, is to establish a life that can be lived after the Gospel, and that for St Benedict means, above anything else, a life that is earthed in Christ. Christ is the beginning and the end of the Rule, as he is the beginning and end of our lives. In the Prologue St Benedict says, 'This message of mine is for you, then, if you are ready to give up your own will, once and for all, and armed with the strong and noble weapons of obedience to do battle for the true King, Christ the Lord' (3). And at the very end he asks, 'Are you hastening toward your heavenly home? Then with Christ's help, keep this little rule that we have written for beginners' (73, 8–9).

Yet in calling them beginners he does not insult his readers by treating them as children, by patronizing them, by protecting them from those demands which will draw out of themselves depths and strengths of which perhaps they were unaware. It will not be *impossibly* tough but it will without doubt be tough. His Rule certainly looks on his disciples as 'sons' but they are also 'workmen' and 'soldiers'. He shows compassion for the weak but he challenges the strong. He is gentle with weakness but he sees straight through subtle self-deceit and evasion. The demands will not be too great and they will be tempered to each, though for some that is going to mean a ladder which leads to the ultimate in self-dispossession. There is humanity here but there is nothing tepid.

The Rule must become the environment in which the disciple has to live, to struggle, to suffer. This is not therefore a legal code set out by a lawgiver. It is the fruit of practical experience, and although it contains certain theological principles it is derived essentially from life itself and sets out to be a guide to Christian living in the practical situations of daily life. What follows from this, as the most recent edition of the text points out, is that the wisdom of many of its provisions cannot be appreciated until they have been lived. Those today who follow it in a monastic community are doing that week by week and year by year. For those of us outside the enclosure the experience, and therefore the depth of understanding and appreciation, can only be very much less. It would be presumptuous on our part to find facile parallels, and to think that living without the vows can be in any way comparable to living the life of total commitment. Yet if our starting-point is the same, if we can say with the novice that we are truly seeking God, then we may turn to St Benedict as our guide on the way, not so much to pick and to choose whatever might seem relevant or attractive to us in our particular situation, but rather to draw inspiration from a great saint and one of the great creative writers of all time. Because his Rule was a means and never an end, because it is always pointing beyond itself, St Benedict would doubtless have rejoiced to find readers who are ready to learn from him, to go back to the Scriptures and to put nothing before the service of Christ.

THOUGHTS AND PRAYERS

> Today if only you will hear his voice
> do not harden your hearts
>
> *(Psalm 95:8)*

With a listening heart that is both supple and receptive
  be open son to the words of an experienced father
  who lovingly offers you the wisdom gained throughout
                  many years.

This Lord has Himself given us the time and space necessary
                  to learn
  and put into practice the service of love that He continues
                  to teach us.
In this school of His let us hope that following faithfully His
                  instructions
  nothing distasteful nor burdensome will be demanded of
                  us,
    but if it has to be so in order to overcome our egoism
    and lead us into the depths of true love,
  let us not become disheartened, nor frightened
  and so ignore the narrow path in spite of its tight entrance—
  that path which leads directly to the fullness of life.

> *(The Prologue, Rule of St Benedict)*

Abbot Lot came to Abbot Joseph and said: Father, according
as I am able, I keep my little rule, and my little fast, my
prayer, meditation and contemplative silence; and according
as I am able I strive to cleanse my heart of thoughts; now
what more should I do? The elder rose up in reply and
stretched out his hands to heaven, and his fingers became

like ten lamps of fire. He said: Why not be totally changed into fire?

(Desert Fathers: LXXII)

> Christ leads me through no darker rooms
>   Than he went through before;
> He that unto God's kingdom comes,
>   Must enter by this door.

(Richard Baxter)

Blessed are the eyes that see the Divine Spirit through the letter's veil.

(Claudius of Turin)

It is not necessary that we should discover new ideas in our meditation. It is sufficient if the word as we read and understand it penetrates and dwells within us. As Mary pondered in her heart the tidings that were told by the shepherds, as what we have casually heard follows us for a long time, sticks in our mind, occupies, disturbs or delights us, without our ability to do anything about it, so in meditation God's word seeks to enter in and remain with us. It strives to stir us to work and to operate in us so that we shall not get away from it the whole day long. Then it will do its work in us without our being aware of it.

(Dietrich Bonhoeffer)

Whenever you read the Gospel Christ Himself is speaking to you. And while you read, you are praying and talking with him.

(St Tikhon of Zadonsk)

> Blessed Lord,
> who hast caused all holy Scriptures
>   to be written for our learning;
> grant that we may in such wise hear them,

read, mark, learn, and inwardly digest them;
that, by patience, and comfort
   of thy holy Word,
we may embrace, and ever hold fast
   the blessed hope of everlasting life,
which thou hast given us in our Saviour
   Jesus Christ.

NOTES

The basis of this chapter, as of the book, is the Rule of St Benedict itself. The translation through which I first got to know and love the Rule is that of Dom Basil Bolton, O.S.B. The fact that it came to me through Dom Bernard Orchard, O.S.B., of Ealing Abbey, titular Prior of Canterbury, is in itself a symbol of the way in which the Rule is common ground between the two communions. In writing this book, however, I have used the most recent definitive translation, that edited by Timothy Fry, O.S.B., and published by the Liturgical Press, Collegeville, in 1982. This is an annotated text in Latin and English and enables me to give precise reference to individual phrases. The index has been invaluable, as has the Appendix giving longer expositions of monastic topics. This chapter in particular owes much to the section on the role and interpretation of Scripture, pp. 467–77.

The Cardinal Hume quotation on page 30 comes from an address given in 1980 at Ealing Abbey and later published in a collection *In Praise of Benedict, A.D. 480–1980,* Hodder & Stoughton, 1981, p. 34. The phrase of Thomas Merton which I use on page 30 I came across in *Simplicity and Ordinariness, Studies in Medieval Cistercian History, IV,* ed. John R. Sommerfeldt, Cistercian Publications, Kalamazoo, Michigan, 1980, p. 3.

I am glad right at the start to be able to acknowledge my debt to Dom David Knowles, whose lectures at Cambridge first awakened in me a feeling for the Middle Ages. On page 31 I have used one of his earliest and shortest but none the less profoundly wise studies, *The Benedictines,* Sheed and Ward, 1929. The quotation comes on page 17. Now long out of print in England, a slightly modified edition introduced by Marion R. Bowman was re-issued in 1962 by the Abbey Press, Saint Leo, Florida.

The section on page 32 owes much to Emmanuel van Severus 'Theological Elements of the Benedictine Rule', *Monastic Studies,* Advent 1975, pp. 45–6.

On page 33 I was drawing on chapter 3 'The Word of God',

from Guy-Marie Oury, O.S.B., *St Benedict, Blessed by God,* translated by John A. Otto and published by the Liturgical Press, Collegeville, 1980.

The quotations from the psalms used in the Thoughts and Prayers are taken from the translation of the Alternative Service Book. A modern translation helps us to see how the psalms speak afresh to every generation.

This translation of the Rule, as also that which I use for the 'Thoughts and Prayers' at the end of chapter IX, is by Ambrose Wathen, in an article 'Benedict of Nursia, Patron of Europe 480–1980', *Cistercian Studies,* 1980, XV, p. 106. All the sayings of the Desert Fathers that I shall be using in these 'Thoughts and Prayers' come from the translation by Thomas Merton, *The Wisdom of the Desert, Sayings of the Desert Fathers of the Fourth Century,* Sheldon Press, 1961.

The collect is for Advent II.

III

Listening

'How great is the freedom to which you are called'

RIGHT AT THE START of the Rule St Benedict had the vivid image of the crowded market-place and the Lord calling out very loudly, trying to arrest the attention of passers-by in the crowd to what is on offer. This is an open invitation, a general offer to anyone who cares to stop and listen. It is not highly selective at all; in fact it is addressed to each of us personally. The Bible of course presents us with some spectacular calls: Moses was alone in the desert, Samuel was dragged out of sleep, Paul was blinded. But then Simon and Andrew, James and John were merely at their usual daily jobs, fishing and mending the nets, and Amos was about his usual work as a herdsman and dresser of sycamore trees. The stories of the call experienced by modern Benedictines are often quite ordinary, reassuringly commonplace. What happened to Paul on the road to Damascus is exceptional; the setting of daily life is far more common.

St Benedict was of course writing for professed monks and there can be no doubt about the rigorous demands that he makes on those who enter the monastic life. Yet never himself a priest and writing his Rule with a community of laymen in mind, his very clear grasp of the principles underlying the commitment of the vows remains applicable and valuable to all who are trying to follow Christ. So however stumbling my efforts and halting my progress, I can still find in the Rule perceptions which support and illuminate my way. I come back again to that crowded market-place and to the offer of 'true and eternal life', an offer open to all, a response possible from all, but with the proviso that if I respond it must be here and now, and it must be with action as well as with faith.

The very first word of the Rule is 'listen'. From the start the disciple's goal is to hear keenly and sensitively that Word of God which is not only message but event and encounter. This is the start of a life-long process of learning, and the whole of the monastery is set out as a school of the Lord's service, a place and a structure to encourage the dialogue of master and disciple, in which the ability to listen is fundamental. The simple word *obsculta* is rich in meaning, for it involves a reverent, ready, humble way of listening. It involves not only listening to the Word of God but listening at many other levels too, to the Rule, to the abbot and to the brethren. We are probably today in a better position than at any time in the past to appreciate just how wide-ranging that exercise can be. The way in which we have been made familiar with what is rather pompously known as nonverbal communication has taken listening out of the narrow sphere of hearing words into the much wider sphere of recognizing signs, particularly in body and posture, and not only in other people but in ourselves as well. Listening to ourselves and learning to love ourselves, paying attention to our body, to its demands and its rhythms, has been pushed underground by centuries of Puritan repression and it is only now at long last being taken seriously again. The ache in my back need not necessarily be dismissed with stoic fortitude as lumbago; it may be telling me about tension and strain, a signal that it is time to stop and to be kind to my body and my nerves and not make impossible demands on myself.

Since we no longer associate schooling only with the acquisition of information we are also more open to recognize the vital part that experience plays in learning. St Benedict's understanding of listening falls into this order; it is the listening of the whole person, of body as well as intellect, and it requires love as well as cerebral assent. And it also involves mindfulness, an awareness which turns listening from a cerebral activity into a living response. Having heard the word, through whatever channel it may have come, even as unacceptably as a pain in my back, I stop and take it seriously and then do something about it. To listen attentively to what we hear is much more than giving it passing aural attention. It means in the first instance that we have to listen whether we like it or not, whether we hear what we want to or something that is actually disagreeable or threatening. If we begin to pick and choose we are in fact turning a deaf ear to the many unexpected and perhaps unacceptable ways in which God is trying to reach us. For example, the geriatric ward in which so many older people now end their days is inescapably full of pain and distress. It would be absurd to pretend otherwise. Yet, bound as most of us tend to be by the relentless demands of the clock and the calendar, we find here a world which accepts another sort of time, where requests and reminiscences repeated endlessly remind us of something which the Orthodox liturgy knows with its continual repetitions again and again and again. These people, a sector of our society which many would prefer to banish and forget, might be speaking to us through their often confused words – if only we could hear them – of that time outside time of which we need a constant reminder.

To listen closely, with every fibre of our being, at every moment of the day, is one of the most difficult things in the world, and yet it is essential if we mean to find the God whom we are seeking. If we stop listening to what we find hard to take then, as the Abbot of St Benoît-sur-Loire puts it in a striking phrase, 'We're likely to pass God by without even noticing Him.' And now it is our obedience which proves that we have been paying close attention. That word 'obedience' is derived from the Latin *oboedire*, which shares its roots with *audire*, to hear. So to obey really means to hear and then act upon what we have heard, or, in other words, to see that the listening achieves its aim. We are not being truly attentive unless we are prepared to act on what we hear. If we hear and do nothing more about it, then the sounds have simply fallen on our ears and it is not apparent that we have actually heard them at all.

St Benedict really drives the point home. 'The disciples' obedience must be given gladly, for God loves a cheerful giver (2 Corinthians 9:7). If a disciple obeys grudgingly and grumbles, not only aloud but also in his heart, then even though he carries out the order his action will not be accepted with favour by God who sees the grumbling in the heart. He will have no reward for service of this kind; on the contrary he will incur punishment for grumbling, unless he changes for the better and makes amends' (5. 16–19). So there is no time for the half-hearted response. St Benedict does not find it good enough that I am not really paying attention to the people who have interrupted me and upset all my nice plans for myself, that in my heart I'm actually furious and my calm smile is no more than a façade behind which I am inwardly fuming.

What St Benedict is really hoping for he has expressed almost lyrically in the Prologue:

> We shall run
> On the path of God's commandments,
>   our hearts overflowing
>   with the inexpressible delight
>   of love.   (Prol. 49)

So obedience is really about love. It is our loving response to God which a murmuring response altogether wrecks. 'Your way of acting should be different from the world's way; the love of Christ must come before all else' (4.20,21).

The outcome of obedience undertaken in these terms is that it brings with it an inner freedom. 'Obedience is a blessing' is the opening phrase of chapter 71 which tackles the question of obedience among the brothers. That simple expression makes the point that it is not negative, not a restriction, but positive and it will lead us to God. The certain conviction that St Benedict established at the beginning of the Rule is still with him at the end: that we go to God by the road of obedience. He makes this clear at the start of the Prologue. 'The labour of obedience will bring you back to him from whom you had drifted through the sloth of disobedience. This message of mine is for you then if you are ready to give up your own will, once and for all, and armed with the strong and noble weapons of obedience to do battle for the true King, Christ the Lord' (Prol. 2.3). And right at the end he speaks of 'observant and obedient monks' (73.6). These are men who 'have learned to compete in obedience to one another' (72.6), and the way in which this is achieved is through the practice described earlier in chapter 7, where the second step in humility asks that 'a man loves not his own will nor takes pleasure in the satisfaction of his desires; rather he shall imitate by his actions the saying of the Lord; I have come not to do my own will, but the will of him who sent me' (7. 31, 32. John 6:38).

That quotation from chapter 7 of the Rule confronts us with St Benedict's discussion of humility, something quite fundamental to his thought though perhaps something which tends to alarm the modern reader. This is probably because our immediate reaction is to think that it means somebody who is somehow limp and ineffectual; in church circles it conjures up the picture of the obsequiously pious, altogether the non-person we should all hate to be. This is unfortunate since the word itself (derived from the same root as *humus*, earth), on the contrary suggests that we should be profoundly earthed, that we should face up to the truth about our human condition. This is a command which does in fact demand enormous strength of purpose. If we succeed it will bring a release of the powers and energy to make us full and free followers of Christ. But first of all we have to tackle what can both ruin our private life and become a corrosive in our relationships with others, namely self-will. It is our self-centredness that St Benedict means by self-will, and it is important to see that when he says 'renounce your will' this does not mean our free will. That is one of our greatest gifts. He wants us to free ourselves from the possessive self, concerned with self-interest, which so grasps and clutches that it gets in the way of any free and open relationship with God. So it is the use which we make of our will which is the point at issue. Are we going to use it to serve our own drives and impulses and assert our independence? Or are we going to use it to serve others and make it a means of returning to Christ? That is the challenge.

St Benedict does not leave us without help here. He offers us a guide to this life-long process of learning obedience. He devotes chapter 7 to showing how this conquest of self can be achieved. His image is the ladder. He presents us with twelve rungs and our ascent is progressive; we must attain the first before we can move to the second, and with every step up each preceding rung is knocked away. The first seven steps look at the growth of the interior disposition, the next five at the exterior conduct which results from that. The starting point, that we should keep the fear of God always before our eyes, is based on something which the Rule says time and time again: we should never forget the omnipresence of God. He is always there, it is as simple as that. God is alongside us – St Benedict tells his monk this very firmly: 'Let him recall that he is always seen by God in heaven, that his actions are everywhere in God's sight and are reported by the angels at every hour' (7.13). This awareness of being a creature of God brings with it a sense of responsibility. If I want to know how humble I am the first question to ask myself is, 'How aware am I that anything I do in any way is part of the working out of God's will?' With that question I consciously place all that I am before God and make him the centre of my existence rather than my own projects and my own successes. That *all* is the stumbling block. Many people go through life without a firm grasp on that first rung of the ladder, a contemporary American prioress told her community in discussing this chapter of the Rule, because they are sure that adversity in

46

their lives cannot possibly be the will of God for them; they will resist the hard thing and put it away from them; they have no room for the recognition that God is running their life. So after asking for the submission of my will in this way the chapter continues, making its demands for radical disengagement. In these first steps the humility comes from the inside; later it comes from relationships with other people. Subjecting myself to another 'in all obedience for the love of God' (7.34) means giving up my power, my arrogance, and instead submitting myself to seek the will of God through others. If I want to grow, openness and interaction with others is imperative since then I can grow with the help of someone else's gifts. I admit my limitations and my weakness, and I let someone else hold me up so that I can go on. This of course prevents any false self-image and cuts down my pride in my own sufficiency. It involves trust, for it means recognizing someone else's strengths so that he can rescue me from my weakness. My attachment to material things clearly has to go, and we shall see later how much stress St Benedict places on this. But equally important, and often much more difficult, is to let go of my ambition and self-esteem, my self-assertiveness, my wish to be just a little different from everyone else. If through all this I learn to deal with my own limitations then I shall be able to deal with those of other people. This humility which I am learning to practise may prevent me from laughing quite so easily at other people, or finding things superficial, or being ready so quickly to scorn and criticize. Knowing my own limitations I have no right to destroy other people for theirs.

The very top of the ladder carries a promise of the serenity that comes with my discovery that God is in charge of my life and that as a result I am finally free. And then it becomes clear what this long consideration of humility has been about. It is the interior breaking free. I am released from my bondage to my self-seeking, my ambitions, my self-sufficiency and all the rest of it. This is of course New

Testament teaching, that in God's service men and women find perfect freedom. It is also one of the central themes of the Rule. St Benedict makes obedience his ascetic practice. Perhaps he knew that it was perfectly possible to undergo extreme mortification, fasting and vigils and yet still not give up one's will and all that goes with it – the tyranny of self-absorption and the self-deception and the fear of failing in the goals that I have set myself (and told others about so that I should fail in their eyes as well as mine, which is if anything even more galling). Only when all this is broken is there the possibility of progress from slavery to freedom. And freedom is what most of us want more desperately than ever. It is true that I seem to be surrounded by enormous freedom of choice (how to vote, what to eat, what brand product to choose when I shop), and yet ironically my ultimate freedom of manoeuvre seems limited, by career structure, by economic pressure, by the expectations others have of me, by the establishment, by the church. I seem to be trapped just when I least expected it.

Yet here is the promise which St Benedict holds out and it could hardly be more straightforward. 'This Rule is not meant to be a burden for you. It should help you to discover and experience how great is the freedom to which you are called.' But freedom for what? 'To be able to do in the depths of your heart what you really want to do' was what Thomas Merton told his novices at Gethsemani. He went on to speak to them of getting in touch with that deep inner centre, using terms which have much in common with what stability involves, 'my being, my reality, what God has willed for me'. The part played by obedience becomes clear as he continues, 'being able to will what God wills for me at every moment is what keeps me in touch with that centre: that reality is the will of God and it demands response. I have to choose, in everything I do, in relation to this. I must keep contact with this centre of freedom.' Perhaps that choice will be very difficult. It may feel like panic at the impossible demand, it may feel like a choice between two

48

evils. Then the only possible prayer is the one that the novice makes at his profession (58.21), quoting psalm 119 (118 (119):116). 'Uphold me, O Lord, as you have promised, and I shall live; do not disappoint me in my hope.' The only hope at this point is to throw myself on the support of God, relying on the protecting nearness to the God of the psalms who reaches out to me just as I felt that I could go no further. For obedience is a risky business. It is much easier to talk about it than to act it out. It means being prepared to take my life in my hands and place it in the hands of God.

Yet by doing this we discover that in fact God has made us collaborators with him, since what he was drawing out of us in our moments of decision or crisis was not blind obedience and mechanical conformity, but rather an obedience that asked us to take moral responsibility for ourselves. Only perhaps in looking back can we see the extent to which obedience has encouraged a process of growth and of self-transcendence. What is asked from us is not the securing of a correct answer but something much freer and more creative. 'The Christian and monastic model for discerning God's will in a given situation is not that of finding the solution of a crossword puzzle', says a recent Benedictine discussion of obedience, 'where the answer must be exactly right, fitted to some preconceived plan. A better model is that we are given building blocks and have to see what can be done with them, using in the task all our intelligence, sensitivity and love.' Blind obedience simply does not come into the Rule at all. Critical faculties are neither wrong nor irrelevant. They are given us to be used constructively and with love. In chapter 58, which sets out the succession of steps by which the novice takes his responsible decision, it is heavily stressed that this final commitment comes after fully conscious, mature and free choice. When he finally promises obedience it has become a free response from the centre of his being, a freely considered choice which carries meaning and authenticity. Later on the monk may find himself unable to do what is bidden and in that case the Rule allows

49

a place for this. 'He should choose an appropriate moment and explain patiently to his superior the reasons why he cannot perform the task' (68.2). If however his superior still holds to the original order, then 'trusting in God's help, he must in love obey'. This grounding in love remains the vital element. Ultimately obedience will come from the heart, and it will be the expression of what we most deeply and truly desire. At the root of obedience is the free, humble, loving surrender to the will of God; the willing obedience which says 'Yes' with our whole person to the infinite love of God, so that outward observance springs from inward assent, a bending of our free will towards the will of Christ, which will finally make us collaborators with him.

THOUGHTS AND PRAYERS

I will run the way of thy commandments:
when thou hast set my heart at liberty.

(Psalm 119:32)

Moments of great calm,
Kneeling before an altar
Of wood in a stone church
In summer, waiting for the God
To speak; the air a staircase
For silence; the sun's light
Ringing me, as though I acted
A great role. And the audiences
Still; all that close throng
Of spirits waiting, as I,
For the message.
        Prompt me, God;
But not yet. When I speak,
Though it be you who speak
Through me, something is lost.
The meaning is in the waiting.

(R. S. Thomas)

Think of it, all that speech pouring down, selling nothing,
judging nobody . . . What a thing it is to sit absolutely alone,
in the forest, at night, cherished by this wonderful, intelligible, perfectly innocent speech, the most comforting speech
in the world, the talk that rain makes by itself all over the
ridges . . . Nobody started it, nobody is going to stop it. It
will talk as long as it wants, this rain. As long as it talks I am
going to listen.

(Thomas Merton)

To the place of your choosing
        I come
emptied of all but desire to know
even as I am known

without words
in the silence of love
my unlikeness yields to your like
your quickening touch penetrating
every fibre vibrating its
        'yes'
to the making
        one

Lord God, patient and steadfast you wait for us until we
open to you. We wait for your word, help us to hear your
voice. Speak and bring your Son to us, Jesus the word of
your peace. We wait for your word, Lord God, patient and
steadfast.

O, let thy sacred will
    All thy delight in me fulfil!
Let me not think an action mine own way,
    But as thy love shall sway,
Resigning up the rudder to thy skill.

(George Herbert)

Jesus, confirm my heart's desire
    To work and speak and think for thee;
Still let me guard the holy fire
    And still stir up the gift in me.

Still let me prove thy perfect will,
    My acts of faith and love repeat;
Till death thy endless mercies seal,
    And make the sacrifice complete.

(Charles Wesley)

Almighty God,
by whose grace alone we are accepted
and called to your service:
strengthen us by your Holy Spirit
and make us worthy of our calling;
through Jesus Christ our Lord.

NOTES

What I say about vocation at the beginning of this chapter was largely inspired by *Consider Your Call. A Theology of the Monastic Life Today*, ed. Daniel Rees and others, SPCK, 1978 pp. 110–15, a book to which I shall be referring frequently. The discussion on obedience, pp. 189–205, was most useful and the analogy of the building bricks was taken from p. 202.

The phrase on page 43 from the Abbot of St Benoît-sur-Loire comes from an article 'The work of St Benedict' *Cistercian Studies* 1980, XV, p. 157.

I found most helpful what Cardinal Basil Hume has to say on humility in *In Praise of Benedict*, pp. 20–2, and in *Searching for God*, Hodder & Stoughton, 1977, pp. 32–3 and p. 39.

Sister Joan Chittister's book *Living the Rule Today*, Benet Press, 1982 made me think much more clearly about chapter 7 of the Rule.

Some of the material that Thomas Merton gave to his novices at Gethsemani has been written up in an article in *Cistercian Studies*, 1974, IX pp. 55–65.

In 'Thoughts and Prayers' the R. S. Thomas poem 'Kneeling' comes in *Not that he brought flowers*, Rupert Hart-Davis, 1969, p. 32. The Thomas Merton quotation is from 'Rain and the Rhinoceros', *Raids on the Unspeakable*, New York, 1966, p. 10. The second poem, as others which I use later, is by a Benedictine nun who prefers to remain anonymous.

The collect is for Epiphany II in the Alternative Service Book.

IV

Stability

'Without weakening or seeking to escape'

THE BEAUTY OF THE RULE is the way in which the three vows, to stability, to fidelity of monastic life and to obedience, all interrelate. Even if we separate them and look at them one by one we shall discover that common themes and underlying threads bind them together, and that there is an inner logic by which they constantly illuminate, deepen and depend on each other. Together they become one great affirmation. They are not, as they might seem at first glance, about negation, restriction and limitation. They are saying Yes to entering into the meaning of our baptism as Christians and into the paschal mystery of suffering and dying with Christ so that we may rise again with him. They involve us in the need to face a number of very basic demands: the need not to run away, the need to be open to change, the need to listen. They are based on a commitment which is both total and continuing. And yet the paradox is that they bring freedom, true freedom.

The vow of stability is altogether fundamental, for it raises the whole issue of commitment and fidelity which is curiously alarming to those in the world who are not asked to undertake the solemn profession demanded of the Benedictine novice. What that entails is vividly described in chapter 58. 'Do not grant newcomers to the monastic life an easy entry' says the opening sentence, and the novice is to be left knocking at the door for four or five days. He is then warned about 'the hardships and difficulties that will lead him to God' (58.8). If he promises perseverance in his stability after two months, the Rule is read straight through to him and he is told, 'this is the law under which you are choosing to serve. If you can keep it, come in. If not, feel free to leave, (58.10). If he still stands firm he is taken back into the novitiate and is tested again after six months, and then again four months later. The phrase used each time is 'if he still stands firm'. Only then does he come before the whole community and make his promises, and then the promise (the word used now is singular) in a written document is laid solemnly on the altar. He has been given a long period of reflection (the contrast with the way in which the church today allows its members to enter upon the marriage vows is striking), and he has had time in which he was free to accept or reject. But then, having decided to accept, he is no longer free to leave the monastery or to shake off the Rule.

The detail with which this process of commitment is described shows the importance attached to testing right from the start whether or not the novice truly stands firm. This is the biblical concept of steadfastness. One of the revelations to the Hebrews had been the faithfulness of God. God is utterly reliable; he keeps his side of the covenant. Time and again the image is of the rock. 'The Lord is my rock and my fortress' sings David when he escapes from Saul. And it is on this that our own steadfastness depends. Men and women must find their stability in God. 'Renew a steadfast spirit within me' the psalmist asks again and again (50.10).

Here is something fundamental to human need. The Benedictine recognition of the role of stability is not a piece of idealism, it is essentially realistic. Everyone needs to feel at home, to feel earthed, for it is impossible to say, 'Who am I?' without first asking, 'Where am I? Whence have I come? Where am I going?' Without roots we can neither discover where we belong, nor can we grow. Without stability we cannot confront the basic questions of life. Without stability we cannot know our true selves. For we are pulled apart by so many conflicting demands, so many things deserving of our attention, that often it seems as though the centre cannot hold. Simply at the level of working out an acceptable life-style the choices have now become quite bewildering. Shall I support Mother Teresa in Calcutta or help leprous children in Tanzania? Shall I take up liberation theology or go in for Zen? Shall I work for Save the Children or for battered wives? Shall I become a vegetarian or throw myself into the cause of solar energy? I may well end up flitting from one to the other until I have collected a ragbag for myself of well-intentioned but half-thought-out ideals based on a confused and superficial amalgam of some of the more attractive elements in each. The danger then of course is that I too become confused and superficial.

Instead of this bewildering and exhausting rushing from one thing to another monastic stability means accepting this particular community, this place and these people, this and no other, as the way to God. The man or woman who voluntarily limits himself or herself to one building and a few acres of ground for the rest of life is saying that contentment and fulfilment do not consist in constant change, that true happiness cannot necessarily be found anywhere other than in this place and this time. Dom Columban Byrne, O.S.B. has written of how for him the greatest thing in the Rule, the thing that changed his life and made it what it is, was St Benedict's insistence on enclosure and stability. He is honest in saying how easy it is to think of enclosure 'as a relentless enemy, frustrating my will, hindering my lawful entertainment . . . the monastery as a prison where everything I hold dear and lawful in this life finds a grave'. Yet he knows that he will persevere in the enclosure until death, and the images with which he goes on to speak of it are of a touchstone, an anchor, the gate of heaven. 'Enclosure is something I cannot cast off, it's the anchor that holds me in a restless sea' for he knows that when he is thinking of escape he is tired of facing himself.

Although they are obviously closely linked the Rule does in fact make a distinction between enclosure and stability.

Stability relates primarily to persons and not simply to place, unlike enclosure which has a more strictly physical or geographical sense. Thomas Merton, although he allows for a most genuine attachment to place when he discusses stability in his *Monastic Journey* is yet insistent that it does also mean the 'total acceptance of God's plan by which the monk realizes himself to be inserted into the mystery of Christ *through this particular family and no other.*' Stability is a matter of commitment to situations and to persons, and since stability can be expected from all of us while enclosure clearly cannot, it will be useful to see how St Benedict understands it and the part that he sees it playing in the life of anyone who is searching for God.

Stability is achieved through perseverance, through holding on even under great strain, without weakening or trying to escape. It involves endurance, a virtue we do not often talk about today. 'If a man meets with difficulties and opposition or even rough treatment, and saying nothing holds fast to patience in his heart, enduring all without growing weary or giving up, for Scripture says: "He who endures to the end will be saved" (Matthew 10) and "Let your heart take courage, yea, wait for the Lord" (Psalm 26) . . . the faithful man should endure for the Lord's sake even when everything is against him' (7.35–38, Bolton translation). So stability means persevering with patience, and St Benedict understands patience in its original sense of a readiness to accept suffering, even to death. This in monastic life takes place in company with other members of the community and we shall see that St Benedict has much to say about making the monastery orderly and stable. But he does not confuse end and means. The good order and stability of the community is the means: the end is that the individual may have space and time to enter into his or her personal dialogue with God.

The balance between the individual and the others in the community is vitally important and St Benedict has much to say about loving each other and above all about persevering in love. One part of such persevering in any loving relationship is allowing the other person room to be themself and to grow. This in the context of stability, whether in monastic community or in family or parish or school, can prevent what is stable and good from becoming static and life-denying. We shall later see how accepting change is the counterpoise to stability. This is made easier for the monk since he has freely and deliberately chosen entry into that situation and has accepted it, and by doing so he is giving everyone, and that includes himself, the possibility of making of it something creative. But so many people find themselves in the situation of enclosure, in a marriage or a career, with the fundamental difference that by their refusal to accept it it has become a trap from which they long to escape, perhaps by actually running away, perhaps by resorting to the daydreaming which begins with that insidious little phrase 'if only . . .' Family life which is boring, a marriage which has grown stale, an office job which has become deadening are only too familiar. Our difficulty lies in the way in which we fail to meet those demands with anything more than the mere grudging minimum which will never allow them to become creative.

That limitation can lead to creativity is something which any good artist knows and it is as fundamental to the artistic understanding as it is to the monastic. It is no less true when practised in the less obviously rewarding situations of daily life. While we can see that art consists in limitation, and that artists must submit themselves to the necessities imposed upon them by paint and canvas, by words or notes or stones, it really is very hard indeed to see how we can apply this principle to the confused and humdrum elements which go to make up modern living: the mechanical repetitiveness on the shop floor, the relentless demands of minding young children, the frustrations involved in being part of some huge administrative machine. Clearly this means accepting the monotonous and making it work for us, not against us. How easy it is to say that! How easy to hear that as yet one more piece of unhelpful moralizing which simply deepens our feelings of frustration and anger! Yet the way in which such limitation can bring both freedom and fullness is the heartening paradox of the Benedictine understanding of stability.

For stability says there must be no evasion; instead attend to the real, to the real necessity however uncomfortable that might be. Stability brings us from a feeling of alienation, perhaps from the escape into fantasy and daydreaming, into the state of reality. It will not allow us to evade the inner truth of whatever it is that we have to do, however dreary and boring and apparently unfruitful that may seem. It involves listening (something which the vow of obedience has illuminated) to the particular demands of whatever this task and this moment in time is asking; no more and no less. This is the limitation which the artist knows when he accepts the necessity imposed upon him and turns it to good account. 'When we have discovered that a necessity is really necessary, that it is unalterable and we can do nothing to avert or change it, then our freedom consists in the acceptance of the inevitable as the medium of our creativity.'

A life of stability is a life that can be contained within the limits of measured space since essentially it is about spiritual and not geographical space. The stability of space and of relationships are all the means towards the establishment of stability of the heart. They are only reflections of inner stability, of an internal unity and coherence. During his stay at the Trappist monastery of Genesee one of the things that Henri Nouwen discovered about himself was just this lack of single-mindedness, or as he called it 'lack of one-eyedness'. He looked back over his recent life and found how disjointed it was, how it lacked any sort of unity, how the lecturing and the travelling and the counselling and the praying were all separate and how this encouraged fatigue and exhaustion. He called this 'the divided heart'. The struggle to impose order on this sort of life-style, which is so comparable to the way in which most of us find ourselves living, meant that he recognized most clearly the very real difficulties of establishing some inner stability. At Genesee he was able to stand back and see the contrast between what was happening and what he really desired. 'Wherever I am, at home, in a hotel, in a train, plane or airport, I would not feel irritated, restless, and desirous of being somewhere else or doing something else. I would know that here and now is what counts and is important because it is God himself who wants me at this time in this place.' He went on to ask himself, in all honesty, whether outside the safe surrounding of the abbey he would be able to hold on to this vision when he once more found himself in a fragmented and fragmenting world.

To wrestle with what Nouwen is describing is to wrestle with the problem of stability as most of us experience it today. Stability in the sense of some geographical space is unattainable and irrelevant; stability in terms of some internal space, that we can carry around, is something attainable, though not necessarily without considerable hard work and perseverance. The ingredients of such stability are entirely undramatic. A few days earlier Nouwen had been reflecting on the importance of sameness. He knew that he wanted to be different, to attract attention, to do something special, to make some new contribution. Yet the monastic situation was calling him to be the same, and *more* of the same. Only after we have given up the desire to be different and admit that we deserve no special attention is there space to encounter God, and to discover that although we are unique and that God calls us each by name, that is completely compatible with the unspectacular, possibly the monotony, of life in the place in which we find ourselves.

The Prologue sets the monk in relation both to God and to man, and for the rest of the Rule an awareness of these two dimensions will alternate. Sometimes the emphasis is vertical, a looking up to God and concern with the *opus Dei*, sometimes the emphasis is horizontal, a looking at relationships with others, and a concern for love of the community. The Rule is also concerned to show, through the daily pattern of life which it establishes, how the monk is both to submit to time and simultaneously to transcend it. The concern for exactitude in the monastic timetable is in fact more than a concern with order. The monk must be at the place of his encounter with God, he must obey without delay in that moment of time because that fraction of time is the present moment, the eternal present, the central point of intersection which is both in time and out of time, and there he must meet God. We in the world live lives punctuated by the constant expectations of a busy life which, from the ringing of the alarm in the morning until the turning of the latch in the door at night, is made up of situations, encounters, demands which we often would never have chosen and would much prefer to evade if we could. Yet is is just within these limitations that we shall find God. The difficulty is that recognizing that and then putting it into practice is simply not easy.

Metropolitan Anthony Bloom asked himself what stability meant in his own monastic life, which has been one of constant movement, and thus one much more comparable to that of most lay people. 'The fact of being limited by a line drawn on the ground', as he put it, does not in itself make one stable. Instead 'we discovered that at the heart of stability there is the certitude that God is everywhere, that we have no need to seek God elsewhere, that if I can't find God *here* I shan't find Him anywhere, because the kingdom of God begins within us. Consequently the first thing about stability is the certitude that I stand before God wholly, immobile so to speak – the place hardly matters.' For most of us the place does matter and to begin with it is not so easy to find God in the countryside than in an overcrowded supermarket. Metropolitan Anthony is a monk and bishop, with years of practice; most of us are beginners. Yet we can admit the principle that underlies his understanding of stability, and which finds echoes with Henri Nouwen. He has found his centre of gravity; he is wholly inside himself. This is the stability of the heart.

When she wanted to help people to find the *poustinia* (a Russian word meaning desert but used in the sense of an inner silence and solitude) Catherine de Hueck Doherty chose the same point of departure as St Benedict, *standing still*, something that can be done wherever you are. What she has to say is illuminating about stability since she wrote out of her own experience of busy city life and wrote for people who were caught up in that sort of life:

> You must understand that the poustinia begins in your heart. It is not a place, a geographical spot. It is not first and foremost a house or a room. It is within your heart. A woman pregnant goes about her daily business with the only difference between her and other people being that she is carrying a child. She carries that secret life round within her, and the mystery of this, which applies to both men and women, is that it is totally there whatever the external circumstances.

The means by which St Benedict expected his monks to achieve stability in its spiritual dimension, which is the centre of that vow, is through perseverance; in fact stability and persevering obedience are two aspects of the same promise and in separating them we have over-schematized what the Rule is saying. The preliminary promise made right at the start, after the novice has been warned of the hardships and difficulties of the life ahead, is 'perseverance in his stability', and his first two months in the monastery are spent living that out (58.9). St Benedict as we saw associates perseverance with patience in its fullest sense of the willingness to give up the initiative, of submitting, of waiting. Sometimes perseverance may be translated as patience, 'those who are patient amid hardships and unjust treatment' (7.42); sometimes as suffering, 'under difficult, unfavourable, or even unjust conditions his heart quietly embraces suffering'

63

(7.35). But the point is made: there is here a strong sense of endurance, of holding on under strain, 'without weakening or seeking escape' (7.36). At one level, as that no-escape clause makes quite clear, this simply means hanging on, not running away, sticking it out in the situation in which God has put us, and in the context of the people whom we find there. But at another level, as the Prologue triumphantly reminds us, it means the willingness to endure faithfully that will involve us in the mystery of the cross. The silent courage, that perseverance, patience, suffering, means first and foremost to accept myself, to know who I am, and not to run away from myself along any of those numberless escape routes which always lie to hand. I have said 'yes' to myself before God, and what follows along that long road, which will finally bring me to the cross but also to new life in the risen Christ, may well be a series of crises, of tests and challenges, with demands so great that enduring them seems to bring us to the point of death, time and again, 'we are put to death continually; we are regarded as sheep marked for slaughter' (7.38; Romans 8:36; Psalm 43 (44) :22). So now we see that that phrase 'participation in the suffering of Christ', which sounded like a programme in the foreword to the Rule, implies a continuing process of holding on against all odds, and that it is not important to get by unscathed but it is important not to run away, since it is only at the foot of the cross that everything will achieve its final resolution and the inner coherence be made plain. Until then it is bound to remain a mystery, a mystery sometimes lived out in great daily weakness and confusion. The one thing that we can hold on to is the certainty of God. Our stability is a response to that promise which reassures us that he is faithful and steadfast and that we should 'never lose hope in God's mercy' (4.74).

THOUGHTS AND PRAYERS

My heart is fixed, O God, my heart is fixed.

(Psalm 57:8)

A certain brother went to Abbot Moses in Scete, and asked him for a good word. And the elder said to him: Go, sit in your cell, and your cell will teach you everything.

(Desert Fathers: XIII)

What is it then to be stable? It seems to me that it may be described in the following terms: You will find stability at the moment when you discover that God is everywhere, that you do not need to seek Him elsewhere, that He is here, and if you do not find Him here it is useless to go and search for Him elsewhere because it is not Him that is absent from us, it is we who are absent from Him ... It is important to recognize that it is useless to seek God somewhere else. If you cannot find Him here you will not find Him anywhere else. This is important because it is only at the moment that you recognize this that you can truly find the fullness of the Kingdom of God in all its richness within you; that God is present in every situation and every place, that you will be able to say: 'So then I shall stay where I am.'

(Metropolitan Anthony Bloom)

The reason for stability? God is not elsewhere.

To fill all things with thy glory, thou hast gone down into the nethermost parts of the earth; for my person that is in Adam has not been hidden from thee, but in thy love for man thou art buried in the tomb and dost restore me from corruption.

(Byzantine liturgy)

Calm steadfast love
   still deep
within your peace
   and keep
our fluctuating hearts:
   our inability
     anchor
   in your stability
your changeless energy
   of burning love.

An elder said: The reason why we do not get anywhere is that we do not know our limits, and we are not patient in carrying on the work we have begun. But without any labour at all we want to gain possession of virtue.

(Desert Fathers: XXVI)

O Almighty God,
who alone canst order
the unruly wills and affections of sinful men;
grant unto thy people,
   that they may love the thing which thou commandest,
   and desire that which thou dost promise;
that so, among the sundry and manifold changes of this
                              world,
our hearts may surely there be fixed
where true joys are to be found;
through Jesus Christ our Lord.

NOTES

What I say here about the interconnection of the vows is largely drawn from an article by Ambrose Wathen, '*Conversatio* and stability in the Rule of St Benedict', *Monastic Studies*, 11, 1975, pp. 1–44.

The thoughts on page 56 owe much to an article by James McMurry 'On being "at home". Reflections on monastic stability in the light of the philosophy of Gabriel Marcel', *Monastic Studies*, 1966, 4, pp. 81–8.

Dom Columban Byrne's description of enclosure comes from 'The values of the Rule most important in my life', *Hallel*, Winter 1979, pp. 187–91.

Thomas Merton's *Monastic Journey* is edited by Patrick Hart and published by Sheed Andrews and McMeel in 1977, and the phrase comes on page 68 from the section 'Monastic Peace'. (I should like to take this opportunity of recording my thanks to Br. Patrick Hart O.C.S.O. for a brief stay at Gethsemani and for a chance to visit Thomas Merton's hermitage: my debt to Merton must be only too apparent.)

The quotation I use on page 60 is taken from Harry Williams' *Tensions*, Mitchell Beazley, paperback ed. 1979, p. 105.

Henri Nouwen's *The Genesee Diary: Report from a Trappist Monastery*, Image Books, Doubleday, New York, 1981, has many good things to say. The part I used in this chapter came from pages 77–8.

Anthony Bloom's description of his own monastic formation comes from an article in *Cistercian Studies*, 1973, VIII, pp. 87–97.

I have taken what I say about the *poustinia* from the book of that name by Catherine de Hueck Doherty, Fount Paperbacks 1975, pages 89 and 93, and page 64 owes much to what John Eudes Bamberger says in an article in *Cistercian Studies*, 1980, XV, pp. 70–1 on defining the centre.

Two further articles which have helped me in this chapter are Augustine Roberts' 'The Meaning of the vow of stability', *Cistercian*

Studies, 1972, VII, pp. 256–69 and Clare Morley, 'A Vision for today in the life of the spirit', *Cistercian Studies*, 1980, XV, pp. 172–80.

The collect is that for Easter IV.

V

Change

'The Lord in his love shows us the way of life'

LIFE SEEN as a journey, an ascent, a pilgrimage, a road, is an idea as old as man himself. One of the earliest titles for Christians at the time of the Acts was 'the people of the way'. We see the individual Christian as a pilgrim on earth having here no abiding city; we speak of the Church, particularly since Vatican II, as a pilgrim church. But we cannot think of life as a journey without accepting that it must involve change and growth. This is something which the Rule knows. For if a central place is given to stability the vow of *conversatio morum* brings in the demand of continuous change. The essential counterpoise to staying still is to be always moving on.

That actual phrase *conversatio morum* has an archaic ring about it, and attempts to render it into modern English are rarely successful. By it the novice binds himself to live out the whole monastic life according to the Rule, in obedience and perseverance to the lifelong process of being transformed as he follows Christ. The reality which it expresses is as old and as new as the Gospel itself, and it is not to the monk alone that its demands, in their ultimate meaning, apply. *Conversatio* means to respond totally and integrally to the word of Christ sent to all of us: 'Come, follow me!'

To realize that the whole of one's life must be open to the possibility of change asks not for a static keeping of the Rule but for an open and free response to the challenges with which God will face us. If the vow of stability is the recognition of God's complete faithfulness and dependability then the vow of *conversatio* is a recognition of God's unpredictability, which confronts our own love of cosiness or safety. It means that we have to live provisionally, ready to respond to the new whenever and however that might appear. There is no security here, no clinging to past certainties. Rather we must expect to see our chosen idols successively broken. It means a constant letting go. It is actually, as so often in the Rule, the living out in daily life of the biblical demands, in this case St Paul's words 'Forgetting what is behind me, and reaching out for that which lies ahead, I press towards the goal to win the prize which is God's call to the life above, in Christ Jesus' (Philippians 3:13, N.E.B.). A modern rewriting of the vows simply calls it the vow of openness.

'When you stop and think a little about St Benedict's concept of *conversatio morum*, that most mysterious of our vows, which is actually the most essential I believe, it can be interpreted as a commitment to total inner transformation of one sort or another – a commitment to become a completely new man. It seems to me that that could be regarded as the end of the monastic life, and that no matter where one attempts to do this, that remains the essential thing.' Thomas Merton was speaking at Bangkok on his last Asian journey, on the very day of his unexpected death. The outer journey, the inner transformation, death itself and moreover a totally unpredictable death – all these threads brought together in this one man at that one moment in time vividly symbolize all that he was speaking about in what he called the most mysterious of the three vows. Ultimately this is nothing more and nothing less than commitment to Christ's call to follow him, whatever that may mean. What is certain is that it will involve dying, and not only death at the end of the journey but the lesser deaths in life, the dying to live, the loss which will bring new growth.

In the Prologue we find an account of a call, a journey and an end. 'Is there anyone here who yearns for life,' the

Lord calls out, and lifts his voice again, 'and desires to see good days?' Then if we hear and our answer is 'I do', God in his love will show us the way of life, and we set out on that journey which will in the end (after we have shared in the sufferings of Christ, for this is no easy road) make us partakers in the kingdom. 'Do not be daunted immediately by fear and run away from the road that leads to salvation', says St Benedict at the end of the prologue. 'It is bound to be narrow at the outset. But as we progress in this way of life and in faith, we shall run on the path of God's commandments, our hearts overflowing with the inexpressible delight of love. Never swerving from his instructions, then, but faithfully observing his teaching in the monastery until death, we shall through patience share in the sufferings of Christ that we may deserve also to share in his kingdom' (Prol. 15–16, 48–50). And the triumphant final words of the whole Rule are 'You shall arrive! Amen.' Here is something dynamic. We discover the real extent of St Benedict's feelings of urgency when we find that in quoting from St John's gospel in order to encourage us at the start of the journey he has changed the original word 'walk' into 'run', so that the message now becomes '*Run* while you have the light of life' (Prol. 13; John 12:35). And at the end he will be asking, 'Are you hastening towards your heavenly home?' (73.8). The response that he is looking for is not simply the response of faith but of action, and action now. 'We will never arrive unless we run there by doing good deeds' (Prol. 22). In chapter 5 he is urging his disciples to put aside their own concerns, to abandon their will, to lay down whatever they have in hand, and to take the narrow road that leads to life (5.7, 8, 11). He warns of the hardships and the difficulties that lead to God (58.8), but he also promises 'more and more progress towards God' (62.4).

But journeys can become a subtle form of running away. St Benedict is no fool. He is scathing about those monks, whom he calls gyrovags, whom he sees drifting about, staying for three or four days in one place, always on the

71

move, never settling down (1. 10, 11). St Benedict does not expect his disciples to wander aimlessly like these vagabond monks. That first call meant a *metanoia*, a real turning round, and our life is now set towards its goal. It will not be easy. Sometimes it will appear as a climb, an ascent; at other times as battle and warfare; the idea of suffering is never far away, and above all the thought of death is always there. 'To keep death daily before one's eyes', (4.47) carries profound implications.

For the mystery of Easter is the crux on which all the different levels of time hang. At one most obvious level it is the key to the actual timetable of the monastery, the focal point of the year, the day which dictates the external horarium so that all times depend on it. Easter dominates the liturgical life. It rules the divisions of the year. It is the centre towards which other times converge. One short chapter, 15, 'The times for saying Alleluia', shows how the monastic life was coloured by the thought of Easter. In Lent no alleluia is allowed; it is the time for penance and preparation. But it opens the way for a whole flood of alleluias during the Easter festival. Each Sunday is a memorial of the day of resurrection, and the saying of the alleluias on that day brings a reminder of the risen Christ. Easter even influences the hours of eating. 'From holy Easter to Pentecost, the brothers eat at noon and take supper in the evening' (41.1). Everything is done in relation to the resurrection; even the midday meal becomes a way of celebrating it.

But this is merely the external manifestation of the extent to which Easter is at the heart of the monastic experience, as it is of all Christian life. That mystery of Christ's death and resurrection is the heart centre of everything for the individual as for the community. Each day and every day we are to live caught up in that great mystery. Monastic life has the Lenten character of a gradual healing of the wounds of sin. The monk 'looks forward to holy Easter with joy and spiritual longing' (49.7). But none of us can avoid the suffering and the passion and the death which have all to happen before the resurrection. The complexity of entering into that suffering is central to the vow of obedience, that total obedience that brings us into the utter self-giving of Christ on the cross. But *conversatio* forces us to consider death itself, or rather the succession of lesser deaths that mark stages along the journey before the final consummation in the last and ultimate death.

We are gently made aware throughout the Rule of the attention that St Benedict pays to time, to sickness, and to age. There is the underlying awareness of the pattern of the seasons and of night and day, and the monastic timetable takes note of this. The hours of daylight, for example, dictate when the services will be said. All members of the community are accorded the respect and recognition due to their age. Although he is quite adamant that 'Absolutely nowhere shall age automatically determine rank' (63.5), he asks that the younger respect the older and that the older love the younger. The younger monks are to be called 'brother' but for the older he has chosen a particularly gentle and pleasing word 'nonnus', which is almost an endearment, carrying a feeling of warmth with veneration.

Day by day, in the saying of the office and in his own reading, each monk will be faced by the biblical account of God's dealing with his people. The drama of that story carries all the elements of our own personal story: call and response, desert and disillusionment, promise and fulfilment, life and death, re-birth and redemption. For St Benedict this is not remote, a thing of the past. It is important that we too know how to read our own history, to see the turning points, the moments of change, the unfolding of God's plan for us at each new step of the way. But the theme of death and new life is recurrent. The dying of the grain of wheat and the growth of the new has to happen to us all, and the ways in which it will happen will be secret, hidden certainly, and quite different for each of us. It may be for a mother the moment at which she realizes that the weaning of her baby is

73

complete or when she first leaves her child at the school gates. Without that separation, which is a small death, the new life cannot spring up apart from herself. In times of the deepest depression part of the pain of darkness is the feeling that it is utterly pointless and useless, and even worse than useless, that it is destroying, annihilating. Only later, perhaps months later, as that inner darkness starts to lighten do I begin to see that here too the pattern of death and new life is taking shape within me. School leavers who cannot find a job and those leaving university who discover that they cannot use their degrees are facing a painful transition, and this is one which is now no longer necessarily likely to happen early on in life; the middle-aged are also facing the shock of finding themselves without employment. Or a change of job for the husband may leave the wife high and dry in a new place, stripped of the familiar and the dependable, perhaps in a situation in which she can no longer use her particular skills and gifts. Then it is hard not to stand like Lot's wife looking back into the past, even though we know that new patterns of life and work grow only through accepting change and recognizing the potential of what is given, not what is dreamt of. It is a sign of maturity to rejoice in what I have and not to weep for what I have lost or never had.

We cannot escape the passages of our life and indeed our bodies insist that we take seriously the pattern of change. Puberty and adolescence are inescapable. Women are no longer so diffident about acknowledging that the menopause ending one type of creativity may open the door for another stage of life which can be equally fulfilling and rewarding. There is no choice in the whole process of ageing; loss is frightening, particularly when it means the loss of much that has been most valued and enjoyed, as memory grows faulty, or sight begins to fail or hearing becomes diminished. Change may be a long drawn out and agonizing process, a marriage falling apart or a breakdown which threatens the integrity of the person. Bereavement itself brings a sense of loss which may at times seem almost unendurable. Yet even here, though this may at the time be almost impossible to believe, new life can come again.

My difficulty is that on the whole I am not very good at change, I cling to the safe and the known. Caught up in the miseries and the confusions of what I am losing, I find I am unwilling to believe that new life is really anything more than a distant promise and that the resurrection is not something deferred, but instead is present now as the key to what is happening in my day-to-day living. As my sons leave home and the house becomes emptier I do them and myself only a disservice by clinging to fond memories of times when large numbers gathered round the family table. I must let them go in freedom, both for their own sakes and for mine, and I must try to turn this newly found space in my life to good account and not simply fill it with busyness to cover up the void. I must live in this moment, not looking either forward or back, or to right or left, but realizing that unless I am what I am there cannot be any growth. If I promise myself that life will be better, that I shall be a more agreeable person, that I shall be closer to God on the next stage along the way, then I am failing to live as I am called to live because I go on dreaming of that ideal which does not exist. The past has brought me to this moment and if I begin today anew I can also begin tomorrow anew and the day after that, and so I shall be truly open to change.

St Benedict will not allow us to evade change, and he has no illusions about what is involved in facing up to growth. *Conversatio* is simply commitment to facing up to the demands of growth and change. One of the specific ways in which the Rule helps with this comes in chapter 4, 'The Tools for Good Works'. There are seventy-three of them, most of them short, sharp injunctions fired at us one after another, without even an opening paragraph. At the twenty-second St Benedict is saying, 'You are not to act in anger or nurse a grudge. Rid your heart of all deceit. Never give a hollow greeting of peace or turn away when someone needs your love' (4. 22–26). Most of these are in fact maxims

75

which concern our interior understanding, the thoughts which control our inner growth. At the end comes the promise 'These, then, are the tools of the spiritual craft. When we have used them without ceasing day and night and have returned them on judgement day our wages will be the reward the Lord has promised: what the eye has not seen nor the ear heard, God has prepared for those who love him' (1 Corinthians 2:9, 4. 75–6).

Towards the end of what Sister Joan Chittister has called 'this long shopping list' come numbers thirty-four to forty-two, in which St Benedict is looking at psychological maturity. They begin starkly: 'You must not be proud.' The real definition of pride is the desire to control; to control my day, my future, the other people in my life, to make sure that the world is put together the way I want it. It is to deny the control of God, perhaps even to take it from him. From this St Benedict goes on to attack addictions, which is of course letting things control me rather than my controlling them. If the only way I can write this book is by getting myself a cup of coffee every hour it is not as socially unacceptable as addiction to alcohol or to drugs, but it is still nevertheless a dependency which limits my free will. Next St Benedict considers lethargy, which is in essence a lack of commitment in that it means that we make other people do most of the work and let them support us. He then looks at grumbling and gossiping which grow out of a negative approach to life: complaining can easily become a habit and one that is essentially destructive, detracting from the value of everything and everyone around us. Then at forty-one, 'Place your hope in God alone', St Benedict starts to look at spiritual growth. This is the contrast to number thirty-four. The spiritually mature adult knows that he or she does not have full control of the world; that can be left in God's hands. Next, by referring all the good in me to God and the evil to myself, St Benedict seems to be saying that as we grow and change we must never forget that we are the creatures and God the creator, and it is through him that evil is to be changed to good. 'Live in fear of judgement day' is the first of four points which follow here so that we do not forget the last things, 'Have a great horror of hell. Yearn for everlasting life with holy desire. Day by day remind yourself that you are going to die' (4.44–7). But then these are immediately balanced by four maxims emphasizing God's presence here and now, in ourselves, in others and in daily life. 'Hour by hour keep careful watch over all you do, aware that God's gaze is upon you, wherever you may be' (4.48, 49). With that established, in the certainty of the strength that comes from the constant awareness of God's immediate presence, St Benedict can go on to give ten tools with the common theme of the seriousness of purpose, set by the opening phrase 'as soon as wrongful thoughts come to your heart dash them against Christ'. And then finally he gets to the list of those tools which bring social and emotional adulthood, asking us to reach out to others, to respect the old and love the young, to make up quarrels and pray for our enemies.

Since he is a realist with a very warm consideration for human weakness, his last word of all is 'And finally, never lose hope in God's mercy' (4.73). It is as though he is telling us that we are to come, through this life-long process of being transformed in Christ, to spiritual, psychological, and emotional maturity, but there will certainly be moments of failure and slipping back as we go. Then if I can say *suscipe me Domine*, 'uphold me, O Lord', and if I am always ready to get up and start all over again because I know that God's mercy is utterly reliable, then I can be sure that if I follow this chapter I am going in the right direction. For that is ultimately what being committed to my own adulthood means. The question that Sister Joan Chittister asked her own community is one I could turn round and ask of myself and my own situation. 'If you are not committed to your own adulthood, if you are just coming in and going out, letting others take care of all the ragged edges of our life together, then you will forever see the problem in someone else. If you want to know if you are committed to your own adulthood ask yourself, "In the last three things that bothered me in this community, whom did I blame?" ' This is no more and no less than taking responsibility for myself.

Maturity comes only by confronting what has to be confronted within ourselves. This is where the vows relate, and illuminate each other. For stability means that I must not run away from where my battles are being fought, that I have to stand still where the real issues have to be faced. Obedience compels me to re-enact in my own life that submission of Christ himself, even though it may lead to suffering and to death. And *conversatio,* openness, means that I must be ready to pick myself up, and start all over again in a pattern of growth which will not end until the day of my final dying. And all the time the journey is based on that Gospel paradox of losing life and finding it. An anxious preoccupation with my personal and spiritual growth is disastrous. The goal of my changing life is not self-fulfilment, even though so much of the personal growth movement popular today seems to suggest that that is so. St Benedict is quite ruthless about the sort of self-fulfilment which is self-seeking. My goal is Christ. And I shall attain that goal only by continuing struggle. St Benedict is no quietist: we get there by deeds not words. Yet the initiative comes from God. We respond and we become collaborators with him. So it is important to see that seeking God in fact means that we give him the opportunity of finding us. Seeking God is not about acquiring something or excelling in something, but making progress towards God through our total dependence on his grace. All through the Rule, usually in pithy phrases, St Benedict reminds us of the role of grace: 'by the means of God's help', 'with the help of God'. With this help everything can be faced: 'Let us ask God that he be pleased to give us the help of his grace for anything which our nature finds hardly possible'. (Prol. 41). God's grace is not a substitute for our activity. Grace evokes our acts, supports them and fulfils them. That expression *opus*

Dei, which is now used for the divine office, was originally a description of the whole life of the disciples, the work of God, something that we cannot handle on our own but only with the help and support of God.

For St Benedict, who could hardly be more conscious of human weakness and limitation, tells us that it is just these limitations and weaknesses which can be surmounted by the all-powerful action of grace, and he turns all the time to this hidden, and often neglected, source of spiritual energy. The God who called us at the start will support us daily and see us through to the end. 'They are so confident in their expectation of reward from God that they continue joyfully and say, "But in all this we overcome because of him who so greatly loved us" ' (Romans 8:37. 7.39).

At the heart of the Christian understanding lies the mystery of Easter, of life gained through death. Again and again the vows bring the monk to the foot of the cross. St Benedict had laid the passion of Christ before his disciples' eyes right at the start of the Rule, as the model by which they were to live. The great central east window of Canterbury cathedral, the redemption window, would do precisely that for the members of the Benedictine community there throughout the Middle Ages. As they celebrated mass and sang their offices in the quire it would be always there before them. For far from being simply the Bible for the poor and illiterate that window is a carefully devised theological statement intended for the monastic community who would appreciate both the pictorial scenes and the textual inscriptions which went with them. Three central panels lead from the cross to the resurrection and then to Pentecost. At the very bottom, the start shows the spies with the grapes of Eschol, the symbol of the eucharist, one man turning away, representing the man who does not recognize Christ, and the other the man who follows him. What that following may involve can be traced not only in the events of Christ's own life but also in the Old Testament scenes which prefigure his passion and are placed around the main panels. Thus Christ is shown laid on a marble tomb: the figures around that scene, supported by inscriptions, are chosen to show what entering into the depths might mean, glimpses of suffering, of darkness, of the pit. For there is Joseph, buried up to his waist and around him five figures with spades. 'The tomb confines thee O Christ, this pool the boy; the boy signifies Christ, and the pool the tomb.' Then there is Daniel, standing in a circular walled enclosure with the walls and turrets of a city behind. 'Daniel suffers the cage of the lion; Christ is buried. One the lion does not touch, the other breaks the bars of death.' Jonah is in the belly of the whale: 'He is held and thrust out, swallowed, shut in the fish: here in like manner Christ is taken, dies and is buried.' Yet from that death comes the new life. Jonah, a fully dressed man, steps out onto dry land and other Old Testament anti-types tell the same story. They are grouped around the central panel of the whole window, the scene of the resurrection, which is the pivot of everything. For it is there in the centre and from it the window still continues upward. First the ascension, then Pentecost, until the final panel shows Christ in majesty, the pantocrator, seated on an orb, his right hand upheld in blessing. '*Solus ab eterno creo cuncta creata guberno*. Alone from eternity I create all things and govern creation.' Christ dominates the window as he dominates the Rule.

For the first offices of the day the light of the rising sun would come streaming through that window. While this for us today may be an aesthetic experience, for the medieval onlooker it was much more. Of all the created things which to them presented the image of the creator in varying degrees, light was the most direct manifestation of God. So not only did they stand daily in the presence of a dramatic portrayal of the paschal mystery; they also lived with the vision of the divine light transfiguring the darkness of matter. So this window is a great affirmation. It simply states in word and scene and symbol what is at the heart of the three vows: that to enter into the mystery, the paschal mystery of dying with Christ and entering with him into the depths means also that we rise again with him, and that this life, lived out day after day and year after year, will in the end make us partakers of the glory of the Kingdom.

THOUGHTS AND PRAYERS

The Lord will complete his purpose for me.
> *(Psalm 138:8)*

A monk was once asked, What do you do there in the monastery? He replied: We fall and get up, fall and get up, fall and get up again.

> Let us live with uncertainty
> as with a friend
> to feel certain
> means feeling secure
> to feel safe is unreal
> a delusion of self
> knowing we do not know is
> the only certainty
> letting the self be lost into Christ.

Lord my God, you have formed and reformed me . . .
> *(St Anselm)*

> I am the part that I must play,
> I am the journey I must go,
> All that I am I must endure
> And bear the burden of my years
> Of good and evil, time and place,
> Before the story all is told.
> All that is possible must be
> Before the concord can be full
> Of earth's great cry of joy and woe.
>
> *(Kathleen Raine)*

God, energy, source of love, bring light out of darkness, order out of chaos, from death creating life. Open our eyes to see, our minds to know, that we may be transformed in Christ, the risen Christ.

> Hunger and thirst, O Christ, for sight of Thee,
> Came between me and all the feasts of earth,
> Give Thou Thyself the Bread, Thyself the Wine,
> Thou, sole provision for the unknown way.

(Radbod of Utrecht)

The Abba Moses asked the Abba Silvanus, Can a man everyday make a beginning of the good life? The Abba Silvanus answered him, If he be diligent, he can every day and every hour begin the good life anew.

> O God,
> the protector of all that trust in thee,
> without whom nothing is strong, nothing is holy:
> increase and multiply upon us thy mercy;
> that, thou being our ruler and guide,
> we may so pass through things temporal,
> that we finally lose not the things eternal:
> Grant this, O heavenly Father,
> for the sake of Jesus Christ our Lord.

NOTES

The accepted text here used to be *conversio morum* but more recent study shows that *conversatio* is preferable. This carries more strongly the idea of continuance and perseverance, while *conversio* has more the emphasis on a beginning, a turning, than on a process.

The quotation on page 70 comes from *The Asian Journals* of Thomas Merton, Sheldon Press, 1974, p. 337.

I have mentioned before how stimulating I have found Sister Joan Chittister. My commentary on chapter 4 was very much inspired by what she was saying and the quotation with which I end that section comes from p. 50 of her book. I also gained much from chapter 7 of Oury's book, which I have referred to earlier, which looks at grace.

Daniel Rees, *Consider Your Call*, pp. 144–53 is most valuable, particularly in taking the theme of conversion and asceticism further than I do here.

In the 'Thoughts and Prayers' the first quotation is from Kallistos Ware, *The Orthodox Way*, London, 1979, p. 173.

I have taken the lines from Kathleen Raine's 'In my seventieth year', *The Oracle in the Heart*, Dolmen Press, 1980.

The collect is for Trinity IV.

VI

Balance

'Nothing harsh, nothing burdensome'

BALANCE, PROPORTION, HARMONY are so central, they so underpin everything else in the Rule, that without them the whole Benedictine approach to the individual and to the community loses its keystone. This is something which speaks to us very immediately in the later twentieth century. The search for personal fulfilment has become something of a fetish in our society today, and yet we complicate our search by at the same time admiring expertise, specialization, professionalization. Total success in one particular area commands great respect. We ask our children early in life to make choices between subjects they intend to master. We acknowledge the superiority of a lifetime devoted to one highly esoteric form of research. Perhaps it is unrealistic that in our day we should again approach the world as a Leonardo da Vinci in the Renaissance spirit of paying equal attention to art and to technology, skilled in every field of human expertise. There is now simply too much to be known and done. And yet it could be valuable to ask ourselves what we are losing, and to set ourselves the task of discovering if we could not, without being impossibly romantic or escapist about it, attempt to become more fully, more totally human, by recognizing that all the elements in our make-up are God-given and are equally worthy of respect. Of course we all pay homage to each of the specialized elements within the social spectrum: football heroes or long-distance runners; the outstanding academic or research scientist; the holy man or the spiritual guru. It is the interrelationship of the three elements that these represent, body, mind, spirit, that now eludes us. Yet St Benedict insisted that since body, mind and spirit together make up the whole person the daily pattern of life in the monastery should involve time for prayer, time for study and time for manual work. All three should command respect and all three should equally become a way to God.

The days of St Benedict's monks were poised on the rhythmic succession of these three elements, prayer, study, work. Four hours of each day were devoted to liturgical prayer, four to spiritual reading, and six to manual work. The framework of the day was constituted by the *opus Dei*, the saying of the offices, the worship of God, which was at the centre of the monastic life. But since the intellect must be fed, and fed by learning and by study, there is room for *lectio divina*, that prayerful reading of the Scriptures and the Fathers, and since the work of the hands also has its place there is manual labour in domestic tasks and in the running of the estate. This was to be the school of the Lord's service: a balanced life based on a recognition that each of these three elements demands attention if the totality of the human person is to be fully acknowledged. The good order of the monastery ensures that each element is given its due space so that the whole community shall work better: in daily living it will become clear that the right relation between the parts ensures the good of the whole body.

Thus the idea of order and balance runs through the organization of the monastery. 'So that everything may be done at the proper time' (47.1); 'everyone is to keep to his regular place' (2.19). Holiness is not to become an excuse for muddle, nor devotion an escape from work. The right ordering of an institution, the right handling of its possessions, the right employment of time, the right respect for its members, are profoundly significant for this is the certain base on which the structure rests. The Rule is to create the favourable environment in which the balanced life may flourish.

Stability, as the Rule describes it, is fundamental. It is

something much more profound than not running away from the place in which we find ourselves. It means not running away from oneself. This does not involve some soul-searching, self-indulgent introspection. It means acceptance: acceptance of the totality of each man and woman as a whole person involving body, mind and spirit, each part worthy of respect, each part calling for due attention. Benedictine emphasis on stability is not some piece of abstract idealism: it is typically realistic. It recognizes the connection of the outer and the inner: stability of relations with those around us (a community, a family, a marriage, a business) depends upon the stability and the right ordering of the disparate elements within ourselves, acceptance and not rejection or denial.

The habit, which comes all too easily to many lay people, of dividing life into the religious and the worldly, the spiritual and bodily, and of feeling that the former even if it claims only a small proportion of time is yet somehow superior and to be kept apart, would have probably appeared scandalous to the man who in speaking of the way to God uses simple physical terms. Here is no ascent of souls, with that visual image of bodiless spiritual beings, which even if their authors never intended it to be so have yet so often brought great unease and discomfort to many readers of that particular genre of spiritual treatise. For right at the start, in that invigorating invitation of the Prologue, St Benedict speaks of us running, of our hearts and bodies being got ready, as though the legs, the feelings do actually matter. A disembodied spiritual being does not concern him. Yet we seem to have forgotten his message, and the neglect of the body has been a serious loss in the religious life of the west. Only in our own day are we beginning again to discover that in our physical bodies we have a temple in which God can be reached, that the body commands respect and carries power, and that to deny this is to cut ourselves off from one of our most powerful sources of energy and strength on our way to God.

When in chapter 7 St Benedict employs the image of a ladder he uses it as the ancient classical symbol of unity and integration. Here it unites earth and heaven, standing firmly on the ground (which is the community) and offering access to God. And the two sides of this ladder are the body and the soul. It is pulling body and soul together, recognizing the place of both, using the two together, that makes the ascent to God possible. For a quite absurd picture of lopsided rungs presents itself if the two sides are not in harmony and running parallel!

This is an integration which many earlier societies knew and which they expressed vividly and naturally in their poetry and their prayer. Amongst the Celtic peoples of the fishing and farming communities of the Outer Hebrides a man or woman would pray 'O bless myself entire', since to ask for a blessing on the soul without also asking a blessing on the body would never occur to them. The two are inseparably linked.

> Give us, O God, the needs of the body,
> Give us, O God, the needs of the soul.

Accepting body and soul together in this way means that a morning prayer is for the whole person, including the work of the hands, in a manner that seems very close to Benedictine wisdom:

> Bless to me, O God,
>   My soul and my body;
> Bless to me, O God,
>   My belief and my condition
>
> Bless to me, O God,
>   My heart and my speech,
> And bless to me, O God,
>   The handling of my hand.

At the end of this great chapter St Benedict says that by the time the monk has finished that arduous climb, and the emptying out process of humility which is what it is describing is completed, that will be apparent to everyone simply by the stance of the whole body. 'A monk always manifests humility in his bearing no less than in his heart, that it is evident at the work of God, in the oratory, the monastery or the garden, on a journey or in the field, or anywhere else. Whether he sits, walks or stands' his bearing will reflect his inner attitude of mind. This might be used as an apt description of the body language which is being somewhat self-consciously explored today, the awareness of how much I reveal about myself by the way in which I walk, sit, use my hands. This is simply the unity of the whole person which St Benedict knew to play a vital part in the Benedictine life, not only for the individual himself but for his relations with those around him in the community.

'That our minds are in harmony with our voices' is a disarmingly simple phrase that comes during a discussion on the singing of the psalms (19.7). It is really saying: unless there is unity in myself how can I worship God? But the question might be extended: or play my part in the community? Or work for the unity of the church? Or hope to promote the peace of the world? The whole schema that the Rule presents brings its definite answer. The Benedictine life can lead to personal integration and ultimately to the transformation of the whole person in Christ.

There are three disciplines or exercises which the monastic life uses which stem from that triple division into body, mind and spirit upon which the Benedictine understanding is based. The integration of the bodily dimension comes through a life-style which commends stability, work of the hands, poverty and good works, observances which lead to joyful service in 'the workshop where we are able to toil faithfully at all these tasks' (4.78). The integration of the spiritual dimension comes through the practice of humility and will lead to purity of heart as a result of practising obedience, good zeal, interior silence, and it will lead the monk to do 'all that he once performed with dread, he will now begin to observe without effort, as though naturally, from habit, no longer out of fear of hell, but out of love for Christ, good habit and delight in virtue' (7.68–9). The integration of the intellectual dimension comes through study and through hearing the Bible, and it issues in pure and continual prayer.

All these however are to be pursued in moderation. In the Prologue in introducing his school for the Lord's service he had immediately continued 'in drawing up its regulations we hope to set down nothing harsh, nothing burdensome' (Prol. 46). The principle of moderation in all things pervades every aspect of monastic life. It is in striking contrast to the desert monks whose ability to sit on a pillar or to do without food for days on end would have little in common with a Rule which even actually forbade the undertaking of any ascetical exercise without permission. Perhaps St Benedict knew too much about rivalry in holiness. At any rate, the members of his monastery received plenty of food, even wine, and in not eating the first meal of the day until the evening they did no more than follow the practice common amongst the local peasants. Even Lent meant only a small reduction of food and drink, a little additional time of prayer, the reading of a special book.

This modest approach to life-style is most reassuring. It is in tune with the ways of simpler living which many of us feel that we should be exploring ever since Schumacher and others have forced us to look critically at how the Western world is using its resources. It brings into focus the tensions between us and the third world; and between the shocking extremes of wealth and poverty in our own society. It also brings into focus the way in which consumer society, with the backing of the media, encourages us on the one hand to eat more than we need, to drink, to indulge ourselves to the point of excess, and then on the other hand encourages us to go in for weight watching, slimming, dieting – another form of extreme.

This same moderation marks every aspect of life in the

community. If corrections have to be made the abbot is admonished to make them with prudence and with love 'lest being too zealous in removing the rust he break the vessel', and he is reminded that sheep may be killed by over-driving and vessels wrecked if they are scoured too fiercely. St Gregory, in describing the Rule as 'remarkable for its discretion', was no doubt thinking of this wise adjustment of means to ends, so that while maintaining the highest ideals it also shows a tender, even humorous patience with human weakness. When you come together for prayer, St Benedict tells his monks, and you start with the Gloria, you should pray that Gloria very slowly because some people might be late, and although there is a penalty for coming late try to give everyone as much of a chance as possible to escape it. This is the moderation which shows a touching allowance for human frailty. It is summed up in that famous phrase: that the abbot is 'so to temper all things that the strong may still have something to long after, and the weak may not draw back in alarm', a level of demand that will not frighten away the weak but which nevertheless holds a challenge for the strong.

The Benedictine climate does not attract or develop a particular type of sanctity; it does not encourage the martyr or the prophet, or any form of extremism. Dom Columba Cary Elwes tells a nice story about a monk of his monastery who was convinced that he was not leading a sufficiently austere life and so left to join another community where the life was to all outward appearances far harder: the monks rose earlier and ate more frugally; the manual work was more exhausting and the silence more complete. He disappeared from view, but returned some months later convinced that such austerities were not for him. They did not lead him nearer to God but left him too exhausted to be concerned about anything, let alone God. He returned at peace and the community learned from the experience.

Neither the Benedictine community as a whole nor its individual members are expected to be working feverishly, consumed with a restless energy which damages health and strength, the phenomenon known in management circles as burn-out, the result of working too hard with no rhythm or relaxation. This is not a Benedictine virtue! Instead there is contentment with the familiar, the ordinary, the monotonous. Dom Rembert Weakland recently pointed out that Benedictines might sometimes be tempted to play down the extent to which their life is average, balanced, normal, by adding a little imbalance, trying to make it look rather more heroic and thus more attractive to the young. Yet that is precisely its strength: to be a witness to normalcy. Though to equate this normal and moderate way of life with an easy middle way which has no room for richness and diversity and would simply spread a safe grey sameness over ourselves and everything around us, is to make a travesty of what the Rule intends. It is insisting on the acceptance of each element in the person, each member of the community, each activity of the day as valuable and significant in its own right without encouraging extremism, competition, over-activity, workaholism. A vision of relatedness binds the parts together into the harmonious whole. We are brought back once again to the Benedictine idea of balance. It can be par-ticularly well seen in the pattern of daily activity, the alternating rhythm which holds the main elements of the monastic day together. The monk moves between praying and studying and working with his hands, going in turn from chapel to library to kitchen or farm. The Rule imposes checks and balances as one activity succeeds another.

When this happens to me I merely tend to feel that my life is marked by interruptions and I grumble and accept it with a bad grace. I feel disorganized and distracted as I am torn between family and job and leisure and the demands of the local community and the organizations which claim my membership, exhausted with travel and rush, with putting down one thing and picking up the next. Can I possibly, in the context of the understanding of the Rule, try to recognize that each of these elements plays a positive part in my life? that each is good? that with perhaps just a small amount more of space, of attention, above all of total attentiveness, to the demands of the moment, they might be able to feed and not to drain me? It would be quite ridiculous to pretend that this could be in any way comparable to the simple life which St Benedict is describing. But still I may find here something important to learn from an approach which insists that a holding in tension of varying activity can play an essential part in a pattern of positive, creative living.

For we need to remind ourselves of this very basic and very modest fact that we are essentially rhythmic creatures, and that life needs this rhythm and balance if it is to be consistently good and not drain from us the precious possibility of being or becoming our whole selves. Unless we take this seriously we are going to reduce the amount of ourselves that is actually there and available to us. We will live with less and less of our whole selves. In the monastic life itself of course the monastic setting, the buildings and their relations both reflect and encourage this inter-connectedness of activity. One contemporary Benedictine makes this point, seeing the life of the monastery as a seamless garment, by finding an analogy in the buildings themselves, grouped around the cloisters, which become a sort of central link-line joining on equal terms oratory and refectory, library and dormitory and chapter house, thus indicating the continuity between prayer and study, meals and work and sleep. Obviously prayer and the oratory are given a certain priority, for as the Rule says, nothing is to be put before the *opus Dei*. But they are not set apart as intrinsically different. For the concept of the monastic day as the Rule sets it out is not based on a succession of alternating superior and inferior events, but on a continuous rhythm of equally valid ones. There is no differentiation between things that matter and things that do not. Instead all activities are seen as significant and are shared as far as possible by all. The relationship of the divine order to the human order is fundamental in the thinking behind the Rule. For St Benedict it was a practical reality rooted in the Incarnation. Therefore he can tell the cellarer that the humble equipment which he handles deserves the same reverence as the altar vessels. Anyone who treats monastic property in a slovenly or careless way is to be rebuked, since all belongings are to be treated as if they were sacred. There is no room for any area of life untouched by God. For God is present and accessible in every moment and in every activity.

While that practical physical setting of the monastic building will not be available for most of us, the attention which it draws symbolically to the relationship between the different parts of our lives remains as something vitally important which we need to remember, perhaps in some cases to re-discover. Even in the smallest house, or in a bed-sitter, we are bound to have areas set apart in which we cook, eat, sleep. Can we not extend this principle and take seriously something which is in fact commonly done in the East, and include among these spaces some space, however tiny it might have to be, which can mark the fact that the areas of our life include room for the presence of Christ. Simply the placing of an ikon, a picture, a candle, an illuminated text, can make the statement that in the interrelated spaces of our day Christ claims a place along with everything else.

For it is all too easy for the varying elements of the Christian life to become isolated, and then to develop in isolation – public worship, private prayer, daily work, silence, study, friendship, leisure and all the rest. The ideal of Benedictine equilibrium is not an end in itself. It is a means for total integration, the transforming of the whole man or woman so that a more complete experience of God becomes possible. And while the fulfilment of that experience will come at the end of the journey when we enter into the full joy of Easter, the reality is also that God is present and accessible here and now, in this moment, in this activity. There is no dualism of the sacred on the one hand

and the secular on the other. Each of the elements of our make-up, and all the life that springs from each of these, commands respect, has its part to play, leads to God. So this becomes a great affirmation. The unity of the person and the equilibrium of daily life which springs from that, is a crucial dimension of the Benedictine vision of relatedness, balance and moderation which underpin the Rule.

Yet I think that the final point that we should carry away from this consideration of Benedictine balance and moderation is the realization that it is no easy middle way. It does not mean playing safe; it is no recipe for mediocrity. On the contrary, it is extremely demanding. Benedictine balance does not mean compromise; rather it is the holding together in one centre of ultimate values, whose force we must accept not deny. What the Benedictine life can show us is the possibility of keeping equilibrium in the middle of polarity. The monk lives constantly at the point of tension between stability and change; between tradition and the future; between the personal and the community; between obedience and initiative; between the desert and the market-place; between action and contemplation. Yet this is in fact nothing more and nothing less than the paradox of the Christian life itself. This is something which is known in the Bible and which the Rule expresses as part of its dependence on the Bible. We discover that things are not as we thought they were. When St Benedict showed his monks how to climb that ladder to God it was at the same time a descent into humility and self-abandonment. We find the same paradox expressed in the gospels and in the psalms, that in darkness we see light; in death we find life; that we are filled by emptying ourselves; that we are happiest not when we receive but when we give. What might have been a tearing apart, a splitting and a fragmenting can become a means of establishing wholeness and balance.

THOUGHTS AND PRAYERS

O Lord my God I cried to you:
and you have made me whole.

(Psalm 30:2)

A hunter in the desert saw Abba Anthony enjoying himself
with the brethren and he was shocked. Wanting to show him
that it was necessary sometimes to meet the needs of the
brethren the old man said to him, 'Put an arrow in your bow
and shoot it'. So he did. The old man then said, 'Shoot
another', and he did so. Then the old man said, 'Shoot yet
again', and the hunter replied, 'If I bend my bow so much I
will break it'. Then the old man said to him, 'It is the same
with the work of God. If we stretch the brethren beyond
measure they will soon break.'

(Anthony the Great)

The whole Jesus demands the whole man.
(Archbishop Michael Ramsey)

I am giving Thee worship with my whole life,
    I am giving Thee assent with my whole power,
I am giving Thee praise with my whole tongue,
    I am giving Thee honour with my whole utterance.

I am giving Thee love with my whole devotion,
    I am giving Thee kneeling with my whole desire,
I am giving Thee love with my whole heart,
    I am giving Thee affection with my whole sense,
I am giving Thee my existence with my whole mind,
    I am giving Thee my soul, O God of all gods.

(Celtic dressing prayer)

God, in all that is most living and incarnate in Him, is not far away from us, altogether apart from the world we see, touch, hear, smell and taste about us. Rather He awaits us every instant in our action, in the work of the moment ... He is at the tip of my pen, my brush, my needle – of my heart and of my thought.

(Teilhard de Chardin)

> In want, my plentiful supply;
> In weakness, my Almighty power;
> In bonds, my perfect liberty;
> My light in Satan's darkest hour;
> In grief, my joy unspeakable;
> My life in death; my heaven in hell.

(Charles Wesley)

O Almighty and most merciful God,
of thy bountiful goodness keep us, we beseech thee,
from all things that may hurt us;
that we, being ready both in body and soul
may cheerfully accomplish those things that thou
wouldst have done;
through Jesus Christ our Lord.

NOTES

The Celtic poem comes from the *Carmina Gadelica* III, ed. Alexander Carmichael, Oliver and Boyd, Edinburgh, 1940, 26–7. For further examples of these prayers and poems see my discussion of them in *God under my Roof, Celtic Songs and Blessings,* Fairacres publications 87, S.L.G. Press, Oxford, 1984.

The story which Dom Columba Cary-Elwes, O.S.B. tells is taken from 'Letter and Spirit: St Benedict's Rule for our Times', *The Way,* Supplement 40, Spring 1981, p. 43, and I have also found useful in this chapter his *Monastic Renewal,* Herder and Herder, New York, 1967, pp. 110–11.

Dom Rembert Weakland's reflections on the Benedictine ethos are to be found in an article 'The role of monasticism in the life of the church', *American Benedictine Review,* March 1981, 32:1, p. 46.

The image of the seamless garment is from Dom Dominic Milroy, 'Education according to the Rule of St Benedict', *Ampleforth Journal,* Autumn 1979, LXXXIV, II, pp. 1–10, and what I say about paradox at the end of the chapter is also influenced by the same article.

In the 'Thoughts and Prayers' the saying of Anthony the Great comes from *Sayings of the Desert Fathers,* no. 13, translated by Benedicta Ward, S.L.G. Mowbray, 1981, p.3.

The Celtic prayer is one to be said while dressing, so that it should set the key-note for the rest of the day. It comes from *Carmina Gadelica,* III, 46–7.

The collect is for Trinity XX.

VII

Material Things

'So that in all things God may be glorified'

ST BENEDICT SEEKS GOD in the most simple and ordinary experience of daily living. He is not looking for any special thoughts, ideas or feelings to feed a religious life. His starting point is simply what one present-day monk calls 'the stark reality of the humdrum'. For Benedictine life is earthed essentially in its ordinariness and its littleness. The fruit of that Benedictine emphasis on the balanced life and on the whole of the self being given to God means that the body has its part to play, as well as the mind and the spirit. The physical is recognized; the material is accepted. Division into natural and supernatural, or into sacred and secular, is thoroughly alien to the understanding of the Rule. 'Wholeness and wholesomeness' are simple and undramatic aims, but they encourage the growth of a Christian life which is fully and totally human.

St Benedict has told the cellarer, the man in charge of the most basic area of the community's life, that he will regard 'all the monastic utensils and goods of the monastery as if they were the sacred vessels' (31–10). Anyone who loses or breaks anything must take responsibility for it, for objects which belong to God cannot be treated lightly, and that applies to objects in the bakery, the storeroom, the kitchen, the garden (32.4–5; 46. 1–4). This same careful attention to all the goods of the monastery marks the chapter devoted to clothing and footwear. These are to be modest and serviceable, and St Benedict's insistence on making sure that clothes should fit properly is thoroughly practical. That the monks are to use 'what is available in the vicinity at reasonable cost' is yet another example of the principle of moderation in everything; neither poverty nor affluence is desirable. It is also clear that clothing was not to be worn until it was in rags and tatters, for there is also the sensible provision that 'whenever new clothing is received the old should be returned at once and stored in a wardrobe for the poor.' So the Benedictine ideal is that of a modest standard of living. There is to be enough but no more. 'To provide for laundering and night wear every monk will need two cowls and two tunics, but anything more must be taken away as superfluous. When new articles are received the worn ones – sandals and anything old – must be returned.' The list of possessions given out by the abbot to each monk is detailed, even down to the minutiae of needle and handkerchief. Each monk is to receive 'all things necessary'. But, as so often, individual needs and weaknesses are recognized, and exceptions will be made so that human need is taken into account. 'The abbot, however, must always bear in mind what is said in the Acts of the Apostles: Distribution was made to each one as he had need' (Acts 4:35. 55.20). Nothing is gained by deprivation for its own sake.

One of the very few things that drives St Benedict to uncharacteristic vehemence is the question of private ownership. It is something he is determined to cut out of his community at all costs. He describes it as an evil practice which 'must be uprooted from the monastery' (33.1,2). 'No one may presume to give, receive or retain anything as his own, nothing at all – not a book, writing table or stylus – in short, not a single item.' He is even prepared to institute a search of the beds in case anything might be hidden there. 'A monk discovered with anything not given him by the abbot must be subjected to very severe punishment. In order that this vice of private ownership may be completely uprooted' (55.16, 17). What he is here describing is in actual fact stewardship. One of the many titles assigned to the abbot is 'steward of the household' (64.21–2), and St Benedict hopes that each monk will equally adopt the same attitude towards the material possessions that come into his life. Stewardship is an honourable word which has recently been so much over-used in church circles that it is difficult to come to it fresh and not to associate it with fundraising. Essentially it should mean trusteeship, the responsible holding in trust of something only temporarily loaned to us for its good usage, and for which we remain accountable to Christ, the one and only master of all goods, property, possessions and talents. After all, we shall die taking nothing with us; nothing is ours to possess by right, our position is that of caretakers.

So St Benedict equips his monk with all that is needed for a decent standard of living, but he also reminds him constantly that these things carry with them responsibilities, they are not owned, they are not to be exploited. Poverty is not undertaken as one of the Benedictine vows, and there is nothing here of the ideal of absolute poverty as the friars present it. Instead we find an attitude towards possessions which speaks more realistically to many of us as we try to face up to the question of destitution and poverty in the world today. For most of us the Franciscan way is not a practicable starting point. The poverty of the third world, and increasingly the poverty in our own country, challenges our own safe and conventional life-style, and yet to give away house and job, books and records, clothes and furniture, would undoubtedly cause more ultimate problems even if the gesture itself was a splendidly liberating one. A Benedictine community today is making another statement. Here is a building with property and possessions, a library, modern equipment in the kitchen, a deep-freeze and a washing machine, paying due attention to upkeep and maintenance and to the balancing of the budget, ready to accept recent technology, prepared to adapt and improve as the times dictate. There is nothing to say that possessions are necessarily wrong in themselves, or, the corollary of that, that the absence of possessions necessarily constitutes something of moral value in itself. Yet in asking that the monk look on nothing as his own, the Rule is trying to establish the mental attitude which assumes that while material goods are to be accepted they are also to be regarded with detachment. This is not, absolutely not, to say that it is wrong to value them, to enjoy them. That would be a denial of the holiness of things. Meanness and cheapness simply cramp our feelings. Detachment does not preclude enjoyment, for then we might be tempted to take for granted all that God has given and forget to give thanks, continual thanks, for that amazing generosity. Ironically this enjoyment and appreciation increases rather than diminishes with the knowledge that this thing or that thing does not in the last resort belong except on loan from God.

The business of living as a Christian in the world without being absorbed by it is a constant New Testament theme. Absorption in the world is the slavery to things which St Benedict so much fears. Christian freedom lies precisely in liberation from the oppressive power that they can exercise. Monastic life, just because it renounces power and possession, and deliberately commits things to God, must have a very special message when the common attitude of contemporary society runs so directly counter to this. Here is a touchstone to which we can refer in the face of a set of values which assumes that the worth of men and women is to be judged by the size of their pay packet or their bank balance, by the area of the town in which they live, by the kind of holiday they take. The Rule is saying clearly and insistently that not only is reverence to be given to everyone whom the monk encounters, but this same attitude (which has of course much in common with chastity, understood in its widest sense as the refusal to possess, to manipulate, to exploit) is to apply to buildings, to time, to food, to tools. All created things are God-given. This is no doubt the reason that St Benedict was vegetarian (though here again he was prepared to make exceptions in case of need, and meat was allowed for the sick who were very weak; 39.11). He is trying to foster an attitude towards people and time and

102

material things which sees them all as matter to be consecrated and offered up to God.

'So that in all things God may be glorified' is not the final phrase from an exposition of St Benedict on prayer, but from an exposition on the craftsmen selling his goods and the thoroughly practical business of realistic price-fixing (1 Peter 4:11. 57.8). There is an assumption which the makers of pious calendars and holy picture cards encourage that God can most easily be found in nature, in a lovely garden or a flower-filled meadow. Thomas Merton was acutely aware of his visual surroundings, knew and loved the blue Kentucky hills he could see from his window and the woods that enclosed his hermitage. But the photographs in which he captured his feeling for the sacredness of his surroundings did not stop at the pile of logs outside his door or the tree outlined against the winter sky. He also paid homage to his desk lamp, his typewriter, his sink full of dishes. The title of this collection is significant of what he is saying about things in daily life: 'The Hidden Wholeness'. He did not believe that men and women come to God through the truncation of their humanity but through its wholeness. 'In this no thing needed to be hidden or excluded, no thing was lower than any other thing. All things were taken up and made part of the whole.' As novice-master he would tell his novices to bring *all* their senses to the monastic life: 'The body is good: listen to what it tells you.' Looking, touching, listening are however skills that often do not come easily any longer to the adult. The childhood vision, deadened or destroyed by the cerebral expectation of most modern schools (and parents) has to be consciously rediscovered. Merton knew that for most of us our senses need educating if we are to see and hear and appreciate what lies around us. Perhaps this is something to be learnt again from the East. The practice of the tea ceremony in Japan shows the sensitive feeling of respect and reverence towards both people and things which has so much in common with Benedictine awareness. Each individual is greeted with courtesy, each object (the small hearth, the charcoal fire, the tea utensils laid out in order, above all the specially chosen pottery bowls) will be handled in such a way as to pay homage to their particular material and shape, and to the specific contribution they make to the whole occasion. Each guest, before he or she drinks, takes the bowl in both hands, turns it and raises it, out of respect and thankfulness for all that went into the making of the bowl and of the tea: the earth, the clay, the potter's skill, the sun, the fire, the water, the tea plants. The most ordinary action and the most prosaic substance have become in that moment an act of worship. Here in this most simple and yet profound ceremony there is time to gaze at things, to enjoy them, and to allow them to reveal themselves as they truly are – just as Merton wanted the things that he was photographing to be able to remain true to themselves.

So St Benedict is saying that material things are *sacramenta*, symbols that reveal the beauty and the goodness of their creator, and thus we are brought back time and again to that simple phrase 'he will regard all utensils and goods of the monastery as sacred vessels of the altar'. We are never allowed to forget that the temporal order must not be despised or neglected. His is a very down-to-earth spirituality. There is no escape here into some interior spiritual life disconnected from the world. God is neither idea nor ideal; he is exceedingly concrete reality and it is only in the concrete reality of my daily living that I am going to encounter him. The difficulty is that most of the time I am so busy and so involved that I simply have not the time (nor the incentive) to see my daily life and work in this sort of way at all. Yet that deeply sacramental understanding which emphasizes common creation, which plays down the division between the sacred and the secular, which brings the awareness that all comes from God, is something which speaks most immediately to my condition and I am a fool if I do not hear it. For it enables me to seek God here and now, just as I am, caught up in all the absurdly down-to-earth chores and demands which I feel trap me day by day. Perhaps after all they need not be such a trap: there is something very freeing about the honest way in which the Rule looks at the prosaic and the mundane side of monastic life.

St Gregory describes a vision in which St Benedict saw all creation gathered together as though in one ray of the sun, all things in the light of the Word 'without whom nothing was made that is made'. Such moments of vision are rare but they stand as a reminder that we must learn to see and to respect the visible creation which mirrors the glory and the perfection of the invisible God. Since the Benedictine life has always been based in one place, anchored by the building itself and its surroundings, the monastic community has never been able to escape all the problems of management and organization which such property and possessions demand. How to extend a building? What to do about farming of the estate? How to deal with the library? With educating the young? These were immediate practical issues demanding answers. There is no escape from the responsibility of being efficient in running a complex community. If St Benedict had a vision of the world as God's creation he also knew that that had to be worked out in the ordinary business of daily living. What we can learn from the Rule is that the sense of God's presence can be mediated through daily work and not destroyed by it. St Benedict can help us to unearth God in our midst. Before I try to impose upon myself any idealized 'Christian life' or undertake any demanding (and probably guilt-inducing) spiritual marathon, I should look around me and see that seeking God does not demand the unusual, the spectacular, the heroic. It asks of me as wife, mother, housewife that I do the most ordinary, often dreary and humdrum things that face me each day, with a loving openness that will allow them to become my own immediate way to God. 'Work is love made visible' says Kahlil Gibran, and love is not doing the extraordinary but knowing how to do the ordinary things in life 'tenderly and competently'. I like these words of Jean Vanier because they put everything into perspective. There is nothing idealistic here. But they ask of me warmth and loving attention to what I am doing which prevents me on the one hand from dreaming of an escape into some form of loftier activity and on the other draws me back from the frantic and impatient frenzy of over-activity which threatens to overwhelm me as I rush from one thing to the next. It is possible, though it is not easy, to make the things I handle in my daily life the means of continually reminding myself of God's presence. But I cannot do it without help. I need to practise this awareness all the time for it does not come easily or automatically. That is why I am grateful to the Rule of St Benedict. Not only does it say 'Hour by hour keep careful watch over all you do, aware that God's gaze is upon you, wherever you may be' (4.49), but it shows me that this is something well within my reach. It is however only too easy to be rather whimsical about the work of the hands, to describe it in slightly archaic and romantic terms. 'The thrill of the work of my hands' bears no relation to what I feel at work in the kitchen getting supper ready at the end of a tiring day. 'To build and create with God, to till, to make things grow' bears little relation to the back-breaking chores that I find myself struggling with in house or garden. There is a great danger of sentimentality in all this talk about manual work and God. God is not necessarily closer when I bake a loaf of bread with stone-ground, organically-grown flour (though my own pleasure may be greater) than when I open a tin or switch on my food-mixer. And yet putting aside all the tiresome idealization and exaggerated claims for manual labour it is still true that work with the hands can give something which is not found in dealing with papers, making plans, sitting on committees. The very act of touching, handling, feeling material things helps to build a small barrier against the torrent of words, written and spoken, which threaten to monopolize us by insisting that they alone constitute reality. Manual work, particularly if it is solitary – gardening, crafts, for example – helps us to know ourselves for it allows the rhythm of the body to operate and gives the time and space for the unconscious to surface naturally. This is the role which Joseph Conrad was speaking about when he wrote in *The Heart of Darkness*, 'I like what is in the work – the chance to find yourself. Your own reality – for yourself and not for others – what no other man can ever know.' The sort of manual work which involves working in company brings other gains, opportunities to fight the impersonal by the care taken in greeting and sharing and reaching out to others. But probably the most fundamental role of any form of manual work is to be a constant reminder of the reality of the Incarnation. The God who chose to reveal himself in human flesh was using one of the commonest materials, albeit one of the most sacred; the bread and wine laid on the altar are also amongst the most common materials of ordinary life. Unless we also give ourselves time to handle the common and the ordinary we may easily lose touch with this most vital truth.

All the activities which the Rule describe not only are equally valid but they are to be shared by all the members of the community. No single monastic work is more important than any other; all things should be done equally well. So the sacristan preparing the altar, the cook preparing the food, the kitchen workers who serve at table, the attendants on the sick, are equally engaged in the work of God. No one, for example, is to be excused kitchen duties, although there is entirely sensible provision for extra help when it is needed – there is no nonsense here about it being in some way praiseworthy to be over-worked. 'Let those who are not strong have help so that they may serve without distress, and let everyone receive help as the size of the community or local conditions warrant' (35.3–4). Care is to be taken over even the most unrewarding of chores. 'On Saturday the brother who is completing his work will do the washing. He is to wash the towels which the brothers use to wipe their hands and feet.... The utensils required for the kitchen service are to be washed and returned intact to the cellarer' (35. 7, 8, 10).

Here, as always, there are no extremes and no idealization. St Benedict proposes a set time for work because he distrusts idleness. But work is to be carried on only at specific hours, and it is to be kept in proportion by prayer and by study. There is no chance here for work to develop, or to degenerate, into activism. Although he does not talk about leisure it is noticeable that Sundays are free of manual work. By breaking off to pray St Benedict is making sure that work does not become an end in itself, an idol dominating everything else. And he is equally on his guard against another danger closely akin to that, work being entirely with reference to the self, a process of self-fulfilment. Work is always seen in its communal context. The point at which the craftsmen 'becomes puffed up by his skilfulness in his craft and feels that he is conferring something on the monastery' (57.2) is the point at which he is to be removed from practising it. The expert is so to exercise his skill that he benefits the whole; he must work in the spirit of respect both for his material and for his fellow men. The satisfaction lies in the work itself and not in the personal recognition that it brings to its creator. The builders of the cathedrals, the makers of stained glass, the monks who illuminated manuscripts are revered for the achievements of their hands, but remain anonymous. Thus for St Benedict work is neither simply a means to an end nor something which has absolute intrinsic value. The Rule has written into it all sorts of safeguards, in the knowledge of how easily work can corrupt and dehumanize; the members of the monastic community will be neither ground down nor puffed up by the work they are asked to do.

Yet ironically St Benedict's emphasis on work has had a tremendous effect on Western culture during the past fifteen centuries. Benedictine monasticism is almost inevitably associated with magnificent buildings, achievements in farming, traditions of fine scholarship and education.

Enormous economic success marked the Benedictine order in the Middle Ages. Arnold Toynbee in fact sees this as 'the grain of mustard seed from which the great tree of Western civilization has sprung', and he finds it difficult to over-estimate its importance. Yet it would be wholly false to St Benedict's ideal (and to the ideal of the Gospel which underlies it) to list these external accomplishments as the justification of the ideal of work. Work takes its place in the Rule as part of the rightly ordered life. That its outcome was to benefit European culture and civilization was incidental, an illustration of what may happen to those who seek first the kingdom of heaven. St Benedict wished his monks to work because he knew that the normal person cannot be always praying or studying. The manual labour of his day involved the hands, and the balanced life that he wanted to establish needed both the physical involvement as well as the mental and the spiritual. Thus work carries as much dignity as does worship in chapel or devotional reading in the library. It has also, like the other two, a similar perspective: it relates both to God and to other people. It is part of the whole exercise of praising God which lies at the heart of the monastic, as of the Christian, life. 'We believe that the divine presence is everywhere and that in every place the eyes of the Lord are watching' (19.1). Work is not to be isolated from the whole life seeking God.

When he first went to the abbey of Genesee Henri Nouwen found that his time in the bakery with the conveyor belt felt like an intrusion, a necessary job to be done in order to earn a couple of free hours to get on with his own work of reading and writing. He discovered that he had not yet learnt to make the work of his hands into a prayer. The following day what impressed him most in a talk from the abbot was 'the simple idea that the praise of God is the criterion of the Benedictine life'. He said, 'Even the price of our products and the use of our money should be determined by the praise of God's mysterious presence in our lives.' It was therefore only in the context of the whole of his life at the monastery that Henri Nouwen suddenly began to be able to cope with the conveyor belt and the bread-slicing machine.

'So that in all things God may be glorified' is the common end of all work in the monastery. If the only point of reference is self then work can easily become all-engrossing, sometimes fulfilling, sometimes destructive, but either way a barrier from God. The second safeguard that St Benedict builds into his community is that work is to be done in a communal context, 'because we are all one in Christ'. This is both a check against unconscious pride and against overwork. There is an insidious danger of making impossible demands, sacrificing ourselves unnecessarily, when it would be far better to swallow our pride and ask for help. Since working hard can easily be made to carry a certain mystique, such protests as 'kept late at the office', 'oh no, not a chance of a day off this week' imply a hint of self-congratulation at the inroads that our work is making on all our other activities. So St Benedict has another warning still: work must be put into perspective with the rest of life. It must be dropped at the right moment. When the signal is given for the liturgy other work must be abandoned. Good order, with all that stems from it, expects that time for eating and time for praying are taken seriously. The importance of obedience to the monastic timetable is to prevent the tyranny of any one element over the rest.

So is work degrading or is it uplifting? Does it carry the curse of Adam or does it bring self-realization? Perhaps these are the wrong questions. Certainly they are categories that St Benedict would find difficult. Yet they are questions of the greatest urgency in a world in which there is so much unemployment and in which much work is deadening, where many people feel trapped by the pressure of bureaucratic administration, where there is a strong preference for certain jobs over against others. Somehow, St Benedict is telling us, we can find God in all this, though it is not easy — harsh and rugged things are expected of the novice, and perseverance means going on making an effort. But it is here and now, in the immediate, the dull, the ordinary situation of daily life, that we must seek God and that he will find us. If there is not always as much joy attached to our work as we might like then the example of Christ's own life (and the Rule is trying to ensure that Christ is always central to us) may remind us that his lot involved crushing pain as part of his creative work, as well as joy. Either may equally be our lot at different times of our life. The vital thing is that we approach our work in the same way that we approach our possessions. We are stewards and not slaves, what we have and what we do belong to the life on loan from God, and it is through that life in its entirety, with all its unspectacular demands, that we shall make our way to him.

THOUGHTS AND PRAYERS

Lord how glorious are your works
(Psalm 92:5)

All that is in heaven and earth is thine.
All things come of thee, O Lord,
and of thine own do we give thee.

A certain philosopher asked St Anthony: Father, how can
you be so happy when you are deprived of the consolation of
books? Anthony replied: My book, O philosopher, is the
nature of created things, and any time I want to read the
words of God, the book is before me.

(Desert Fathers: CIII)

Wealth consists not in having great possessions but in
having few wants.

Forth in thy Name, O Lord I go
My daily labour to pursue:
Thee, only thee, resolved to know,
In all I think, or speak, or do.

The task thy wisdom hath assign'd
O let me cheerfully fulfil:
In all my works thy presence find,
And prove thy good and perfect Will.

(Charles Wesley)

Lift up the stone and you will find me,
cleave the wood and I am there.
He that wonders shall reign.

(Oxyrynchus Papyrus)

One of the elders said: If a man settles in a certain place and does not bring forth the fruit of that place, the place itself casts him out, as one who has not borne its fruit.

(Desert Fathers: LIV)

> Bless O God my little cow
> > Bless O God my desire;
> Bless Thou my partnership
> > And the milking of my hands, O God.
>
> Bless O God each teat
> > Bless O God each finger;
> Bless Thou each drop
> > That goes into my pitcher, O God.

(Celtic milking song)

The Word of God who is God wills in all things and at all times to work the mystery of His embodiment.

(Maximus the Confessor)

> Almighty God,
> you have created the heavens and
> > the earth,
> and made man in your own image.
> Teach us to discern your hand in all
> > your works,
> and to serve you with reverence and
> > thanksgiving;
> through Jesus Christ our Lord
> who with you and the Holy Spirit
> > reigns supreme over all things
> now and forever.

NOTES

The phrase at the start of this chapter comes from Kevin Fogarty in *Hallel*, Winter 1979, and that about 'wholeness and wholesome' from Dame Paula Fairlie in *A Touch of God, Eight Monastic Journeys*, ed. Maria Boulding, SPCK, 1982, p. 115.

Thomas Merton's photographs are published in *A Hidden Wholeness: The Visual World of Thomas Merton*, ed. John Howard Griffin, Houghton Mifflin Co., Boston, 1970, paperback edition 1979. The actual quotation comes on page 10 of the introduction.

My description of the Japanese tea ceremony is based on personal experience, but anyone interested in reading more about it will find a most full and useful account in Horst Hammitzsch, *Zen in the Art of the Tea Ceremony*, translated Peter Lemesurier, Penguin, 1982.

The words of Jean Vanier come from *Community and Growth*, Darton, Longman and Todd, 1979, p. 220.

The Arnold Toynbee discussion of the Benedictine contribution by the reconsecration of work came from *Man at Work in God's World*, papers delivered at the Church and Work congress held in Albany, New York, 1955, and subsequently published by Longmans, Green and Co, 1956. I owe this reference to Canon Sam Van Culin.

Henri Nouwen's account of his time on the conveyor belt is on page 28 of the *Genesee Diary*.

In 'Thoughts and Prayers' the Celtic Milking Song is taken from *Carmina Gadelica* IV, 64–5. It is only one of many I might have chosen, but I like it for its immediacy about working with the hands.

The collect comes from the Alternative Service Book for the fifth Sunday before Advent.

VIII

People

'We are all one in Christ'

THE PRESENCE OF CHRIST is felt throughout the Rule, the immediate and central reality of the Benedictine life, as the redemption window in Canterbury would continually remind its monastic community; Christ crucified, risen, ascended, the governor of all creation was always before their eyes. The Rule presents no abstract or remote theological treatise on God and his mysteries. Instead it is pervaded with the idea of sacramental encounter with Christ in the circumstances of daily life and in material things, but most particularly in people. For St Benedict was a Christ-man: Christ was for him the whole meaning of the Christian life, from start to finish. Without Christ nothing makes sense; with Christ all things are possible. That favourite phrase of his, 'for the love of Christ', says it all. So we meet Christ everywhere in the monastery, and in the monastery we return to God by following the Gospel, which of course means Christ.

St Benedict finds Christ in people: in the brothers, in guests, in the invalid however tiresome, in strangers and travellers, but above all in the abbot who in himself reflects Christ whose place he takes as the father of his monks. Not that the abbot *is* Christ, but that he is to be regarded as Christ just as much as the traveller, the sick brother, the guest. Since Christ is the key it is only in him and through him that we begin to understand questions of relationships, of authority, of community. So we are not faced with issues of some abstract moral law, but rather with our own loving response to Christ's own love to us. Since 'we are all one in Christ' Christ and community are linked. 'Let them prefer nothing whatever to Christ, and may he bring us *all* together to everlasting life' (Ephesians 6:8, 2:20, 72.11).

The Rule starts from human nature as it is and not from any false idealism. The mention which St Benedict gives in passing, in chapter 2, of some of the more troublesome members of the community has the ring of reality about it. Some are stubborn and dull, undisciplined and restless, others negligent and disdainful (there are of course also the obedient and docile and patient). There are the stupid and the lazy, the careless and the scatterbrained, and those who are always getting in the way, only too familiar in any group or organization or parish. We know the picture only too well. But this is how we are, and we are just those people whom St Benedict will try to lead to God. Endlessly the Rule makes room for each individual to grow in holiness at his or her own speed, in his or her own way. The Rule is devised for people, the community exists for the sake of the individual, and not vice versa. It is in the sections that might at first seem most dated, the instructions to the servers, the cellarer, the door-keeper and so on, that in fact we can see this most clearly. Here we are presented with detailed and careful regulations about the minutiae of corporate life, and here we find what firmness, discretion, and humanity St Benedict displays. He shows how the well-organized community life makes possible the growth of the individual, knowing that a well-ordered life-style is more likely to encourage holiness than a badly-organized one. But he never confuses public order and private holiness. He insists that things should be done in such a way as to cause minimum irritation or inconvenience to others because he recognizes the demands of privacy, the rights of the individual, and at a more profound theological level that 'the only person who has rights over the inner life of another person is God Himself . . . growth is not something which can be manipulated by human rules or ideologies; maturity cannot be mass produced.' The way of St Benedict simply makes space for the individual seeking God to find him in his or her own way. Chapter 40, which deals with the drinking of wine, opens with a quotation from 1 Corinthians: 'Each man has his special gift from God, one of one kind, another of another kind.' St Benedict then goes on to say that although it is more becoming for monks not to drink he will make allowance for those unable to abstain. This really says a lot about his sensitivity to people, for he is offering a basis on which each individual can grow and develop. He has no interest in mediocre uniformity. So St Benedict approaches the common life of the community with a benevolent recognition of individual personal need and potential. He hopes that all will be patient of the weaknesses of others, he prefers mercy to justice, he looks for consideration of one another, and above all he places love before zeal.

The outcome of this is that the Rule shows respect for each single person whoever they may be, irrespective of class, background, professional skill. This totally cuts through the sham that any one person is superior to any other or could have more value than another. Without being a revolutionary or a subversive St Benedict quietly challenged the preconceptions of his day and questioned much that was generally accepted in the ordering of society. A man born free is not to be given higher rank than a slave (2.18); care and concern is to be given to the poor most specially, because he knows that the natural tendency is to revere the rich (53.15); priestly dignity in itself constitutes no claim to special status (60); age is never automatically to determine rank, and the junior brothers are to be listened to seriously because 'the Lord often reveals what is better to the younger' (3.3). There is a nice touch about welcoming visiting monks (and it is after all those in the same line of business who can be the most threatening) and encouraging them to stay so that others may benefit from their presence 'because wherever we may be, we are in the service of the same Lord' (61.10).

117

The section of the Rule which deals with forms of address is really a short treatise on good manners, that old-fashioned virtue, which assumes that courtesy is due to everyone in an appropriate form. The loving forms of greeting which show charity and esteem are no more, as so often in the Rule, than the practical expression of a biblical injunction: 'They should each try to be the first to show respect to the other' (Romans 12:10. 63. 10–17).

So St Benedict's brothers live together as equals, sharing the same dress, food, possessions and moreover all sharing equally in the round of community work. It is perhaps a little difficult to appreciate what an extraordinary achievement this would have been in St Benedict's own day. Work, held in low esteem, has become a common bond amongst his monks, a bridge between the members of the educated and governing classes, who would have despised it, and the slaves, who would have performed it, outside the monastic walls. The respect for people and the respect for the work they do and the things they handle inter-connect and deepen each other. If the Rule says that the gardening tools are as worthy of attention as the altar vessels, then it should follow that those who deal with them are also worthy of equal respect. The implications of this in modern terms are quite far-reaching. My own preference is for books rather than for petrol, to take an absurd example, which I am sure many others would reverse. And if I am totally honest with myself it means that I have, perhaps quite subconsciously, a greater respect for a writer or lecturer than for the man or woman who manages a garage and sells me petrol. If I take the Rule seriously it forces me to notice this, and if I am trying to live by it, it forces me to re-think my attitudes.

It is just because we are accepted by Christ that we can accept others and accept ourselves. Self-love is important, fundamentally important. The novice begins with the process of stripping himself, or letting himself be stripped of the empirical self, so that the real self may emerge in the common life of the community, which is the school of love.

In this school of love three dimensions of love grow together: love of self, love of the brethren, love of God. To know myself without any complacency and without any self-justification means really loving myself, knowing myself as I really am, set free from wishful thinking. Only after that honesty, standing naked before the God who loves, accepts and does not judge, can I turn and present that same image, stripped of all false colours, to all the other people in my life.

Once again it is the vows which are illuminating here. If stability means that I do not run away from myself it will also help me to see others as they really are and allow them to be their authentic selves rather than the selves I might prefer. The practice of obedience means that I lay aside idols, and empty myself at my centre, so that I can reach out to others. And above all openness to growth means that I bring some dynamic quality of love into relationships, so that I am ready to change, to renew the pattern of marriage, to encourage my children to grow into freedom, to work at a friendship to prevent it fossilizing at some past stage of my life.

St Benedict is a realist about loving as about so many fundamentals. He knows that it is not easy and that it only comes with practice. He does not describe the common life in glowing terms, nor find the rather romantic attraction to it of St Augustine: 'How good it is, how sweet, to dwell together as brothers. These words of the psalm, this chant full of sweetness, this ravishing melody . . . has inspired brethren to dwell together; this verse has been a clarion call to them.' St Benedict gives one superb chapter on love, chapter 72, right at the very end of the Rule, and only then does he speak of fervent love and pure love and humble love as the ideals. The foundation of this love is that daily, ordinary practice of loving with which the Rule is underlined. To see the face of Christ in all those whom we meet day in day out is never easy. It often asks from us patience, imagination, good humour. St Benedict does not approach this with any abstract principle; rather he gives practical examples of what loving involves.

His instructions to the porter are thoroughly down to earth. 'As soon as anyone knocks, or a poor man calls out, he replies, "Thanks be to God" or "Your blessing, please"; then, with all the gentleness that comes from the fear of God, he provides a prompt answer with the warmth of love' (66. 3–4). Here is a glimpse of the reality of love in action. It is only too easy to keep the lines 'Let everyone that comes be received as Christ' pinned up above the sink in the kitchen as some sort of pleasing pious ideal; it is very much more difficult, whenever the doorbell rings or the telephone goes or people arrive unexpectedly for a meal, for me actually to *be* there, and to put that into practice by greeting them with my whole self. That asks a lot, and the Rule knows this and has wise advice about the exercise of hospitality.

For 'Let everyone that comes be received as Christ', that most familiar phrase of the Rule, at once says that hospitality means more than simply the open door, and the place at table; it means warmth, acceptance, enjoyment in welcoming whoever has arrived. And yet at the same time the Rule in its wisdom hedges this ideal with safeguards to ensure that we do not become like Martha, harassed and harried, and as a consequence resentful, so drained that hospitality has become counter-productive.

For hospitality brings us back to the theme of acceptance, accepting ourselves and accepting others, in a most immediate and practical situation which we cannot evade. There is a knock at the door and I have to respond; as I lay four extra places for supper I know that soon four people will be sitting round the table sharing the meal. If I am actually afraid and defensive (or aggressive, which is much the same), anxious and insecure about the impression that I shall be making, I may offer a glass of sherry or a bowl of soup but any real hospitality of the heart will be lacking; I shall have merely fulfilled the social expectation. I cannot become a good host until I am at home in my own house, so rooted in my centre (as stability has taught) that I no longer need to impose my terms on others but can instead afford to offer them a welcome that gives them the chance to be completely themselves. Here again is the paradox, that by emptying myself I am not only able to give but also to receive. Filled with prejudice, worry, jealousy, I have no inner space to listen, to discover the gift of the other person, to take down my defences and be open to what they have to offer.

But there is another danger, and that is that I may be so welcoming and so ready to give that I give too much of myself. The cheerful greeting is right and St Benedict is insistent that the porter is always ready with his warm response. The ritual of the kiss of peace and the sharing of food has its modern counterpart. But this most genuine and loving reception is balanced by a very serious attention on the part of the Rule to the vital importance of protecting the peace and silence of the monastery against any intrusion that might unduly disturb its order. St Benedict is careful to impose limits so that the life and work of the monastery can go on – and that of course will ensure that the guest experiences the place as it truly is. Too great a merging of monks and guest will benefit neither. The liturgy after all is pointing to the same principle. Time and space must always be kept so that the monk can encounter God. A proper care and love of myself is something I must preserve at all costs, even in the face of the subversive claims that I hear so many other people making about how they never spare themselves and how they never count the cost in what they do for others. Endless people encountered, a mass of entertaining, constant coming and going, countless numbers of people and at the end of all this activity St Benedict faces us with two very simple questions: Did we see Christ in them? Did they see Christ in us?

For if we are really to receive everyone as Christ that means that we must respect each as made in the image of God and not in the image of ourselves. And this particular piece of idolatry is all too easy. Unless I am careful I am tempted to manipulate the people in my life (and here this is not simply the guests but my own family, my friends and colleagues, even casual acquaintances). I find that I batter them with my demands, or force my own expectations upon them or so influence them that they feel bound to act in a way that they know will please me. I have in fact failed to accept them as they really are. I have not been content simply to be alongside them in their littleness and their weakness, their frustration and their depression. Perhaps I have tried to improve them or organize them for their own good. Perhaps I have really been much more concerned with where I am myself than with seeing where they are, and revealing *their* importance, to themselves and to me. Instead I have judged them and stifled them, and in doing this I have been devaluing them, using them to my own advantage.

This asks of me restraint and sensitivity, a restraint that is comparable to chastity taken in its widest sense of meaning the refusal to use another person as an instrument for my own pleasure or self-gratification. There is no Benedictine vow of chastity; the word practically does not occur in the Rule and the concept is never treated as such apart from the inclusion of the command 'love chastity' in chapter four. 'The pure love of brothers' is a phrase used in passing in chapter 72, a chapter which speaks of warmth, forbearance, humanity between the brethren and whose tone is set by a text from Romans, 'They should each try to be the first to show respect to the other' (Romans 12:10.72.4). On the day of his profession the novice gives away any possessions he might have 'without keeping back a single thing for himself, well aware that from that day he will not have even his own body at his disposal' (58. 24–25). This is not a denial of the body, for that would be quite contrary to the whole Benedictine way, but it is listed with all his other property and possessions and so the same principle of trusteeship and stewardship applies here too. So sex does not appear as a subject to be treated in isolation, it appears as an integral part of the nature of the whole person and in the context of

122

the theme of respect and reverence that marks the Rule at every turn. This is in striking contrast to the present-day approach to the subject of sex which tends to isolate it, handling it as something which can be dealt with in its own right, self-consciously set apart by the parent or teacher who first broaches it as a topic of the greatest significance, something to be looked at with due seriousness at the appropriate age. Yet how can I as a mother expect a teenage son or daughter to treat their bodies with reverence, suddenly at some point in their adolescence, unless they know this already as something experienced in their childhood world in relation to toys and food and animals? If we have been handling their bodies with a tired and angry impatience, wrenching their clothes over their heads, dragging them in and out of the bath, trailing them with frustration round the shops, then right from the start we have been guilty of making a statement, however unconsciously, about the dignity of the body. Of course there is infinitely more to sexual attitudes and behaviour than this; here is the starting point of respect and responsibility. But all the same it is a refreshing corrective to our near obsession with sex in its every aspect that St Benedict chose to take it in his stride as something not to be isolated as one element in the individual make-up. Instead he sees it as something which is essentially part of the total life of loving and being loved, accepting and being accepted, without which we can none of us become fully human beings made in the image of Christ.

The monk in his community must be able to find both human and divine love. 'Love is the driving force in a monk's life, and the community is there to sustain him in his love for God and to give him the chance to realize it effectively in loving and being loved by his brethren.' Here he experiences the certainty that he is needed, accepted, forgiven; this is the ground of monastic friendship. Friendship is a much neglected art, which receives less attention today than does either marriage or the family. One of the favourite words the church uses to describe itself is a family.

Yet it should be honestly admitted that that image so often conjures up a picture of young marrieds with young children, a model that excludes and thereby wounds the majority of the human race. Those who are single, those who are part of a broken or a dispersed family, depend upon the warmth and support that comes from friendship. The monastic life, with its acceptance of celibacy, does not preclude such warm relationships, rather it makes them more free and open simply because it does not equate loving with sex. This is not in any way to deny affective sexuality; it is simply that it should not be equated with physical, sexual intimacy. 'The sexual urge is God-given. It gives a dimension and force to everything we think and do, including our prayer. It is an urge to give myself as fully as I can. It is an integral part of companionship, of love and living.' Thus a present-day monk. But our Western culture has tended to impoverish this by equating our attitude to love and affection with the physical, especially with the genital. Men and women must have friendship. I need both men and women friends in my life. I need to love and to accept love in return. This is as true for those who are married and who need to keep up friendships outside of marriage as it is for those who are single. Love, trust, acceptance – these are things that I receive from Christ, and it is only as I come to know and to love Christ and to realize that I am known and loved, that I can also love my fellows. My primary relationship is with Christ: it is through him that I forge my link with others, and that gradually I grow towards maturity in loving, in the giving and receiving of love.

THOUGHTS AND PRAYERS

Know that the Lord he is God: it is he who has
made us, and not we ourselves; we are his people
(Psalm 100:2)

Your way of acting should be different from the
world's way: the love of Christ must come before all else.
You are not to act in anger
or nurse a grudge.
Rid your heart of all deceit.
Never give a hollow greeting of peace
or turn away when someone needs your love.
(Rule of St Benedict 4:20–26)

A man who, while remembering God, respects every
man, by a hidden movement of God's hand himself
receives help from every man. A man who protects the
injured has God as his helper; a man who stretches his
hand to aid his brother has God's arm to support him.
(Isaac of Syria)

Continue to keep a warm love for me. . . . I cannot be
with you physically but my heart is always with you.
Like me make efforts to win friends everywhere. . . .
Do not think you will ever have enough. Be bound to
all, whether rich or poor, in brotherly sympathy. This
letter is a document of the heart.
(St Anselm writing from Canterbury to Bec in 1093)

Build we each the other up:
Pray we for our faith's increase,

Lasting comfort, steadfast hope,
  Solid joy and settled peace.
More and more let love abound:
  Never, never may we rest,
Till we are in Jesus found,
  Of our paradise possessed.

(Charles Wesley)

Husband and wife characteristically accept each other as they are. Their faith in each other's regard for them is not based on their own worth or right, but on the other's acceptance of them just as they are. It is hard to think of any other relationship (except perhaps within a religious community) where acceptance could be so unreserved, so productive of mutual health and growth.

> Beloved
>   let us love
>   for the loving
>   is the sending
>   and the mending
>   and the end
>   of the strife-hate
>   in the heart of man
>   Christ love
>   Abba

The essence of prayer is to hear the voice of another, of Christ, but likewise to hear the voice of each person I meet in whom Christ also addresses me. His voice comes to me in every human voice, and his face is infinitely varied. It is present in the face of the wayfarer on the road to Emmaus; it is present in the gardener speaking to Mary Magdalen, it is present in my next-door neighbour. God became incarnate so that man might contemplate his face in every face. Perfect prayer seeks this presence of Christ and recognizes it in every human face. The unique image of Christ is the ikon, but every human face is an ikon of Christ, discovered by a prayerful person.

(Catherine de Hueck Doherty)

Almighty Father,
whose Son Jesus Christ has taught us
that what we do for the least of our brethren
   we do also for him;
give us the will to be the servant of others
   as he was the servant of all,
who gave up his life and died for us,
but is alive and reigns with you and the Holy Spirit,
one God, now and for ever.

NOTES

The quotation on pages 116–17 comes from an article that I have mentioned before, Dominic Milroy, 'Education according to the Rule of St Benedict', *Ampleforth Journal*, Autumn 1979, LXXXIV, p. 2.

What I say at the top of page 119 is drawn from a piece by Charles Dumont, but I have failed to trace the reference.

The extract from St Augustine was used by Oury in chapter 10 of his book which deals with community.

I much enjoyed Henri Nouwen, 'The poverty of a host', *Monastic Studies*, No. 10, Easter 1974, pp. 65, 69.

Two short paragraphs on p. 126 of *Consider Your Call* speak most wisely about friendship, and the quotation on page 124 is taken from the chapter by Dom Dominic Gaisford in *A Touch of God*, p. 164.

I found useful for page 118 Bernard Ducruet's 'The Work of St Benedict', *Cistercian Studies*, 1980, XV, 2, pp. 152–61.

In 'Thoughts and Prayers', the quotation about husband and wife is taken from the report *Marriage, Divorce and the Church*, SPCK 1971, pp. 33–4, and that by Catherine de Hueck Doherty from her book *Poustinia*, p. 92, which I mentioned earlier in the chapter on Stability.

The collect is that of the Alternative Service Book for Pentecost 11 (Trinity 10).

IX

Authority

'the utmost care and concern'

'ADVICE FROM A FATHER who loves you', a phrase in the second sentence of the Rule, follows immediately the opening sentence 'Listen carefully, my son, to the master's instructions' and qualifies it. The juxtaposition of the two is significant; it sets the scene from the start. Here is authority of a master exercised with the loving solicitude of a father. So the first thing that defines the abbot is not his position at the head of an institution but his relationship with sons. The way in which this was lost in the Middle Ages when the abbot became less and less the loving father and more and more the wealthy, industrious prelate, administrator and public figure, only helps to make the point that this type of leadership demands constant watching if it is not to become institutionalized, the structure taking precedence over people. But this is not the *pater familias* of the later Roman society, the role which gave the head of his household control over his slaves and children to the point of life and death. To see it in terms of a patriarchal relationship is to miss much that is sensitive, and we today, as we question the Victorian father-figure and yet cannot find a wholly adequate alternative, are well placed to appreciate this. But the fullness of the portrait can only really emerge when we add to it the other titles which the Rule gives to the abbot, master and shepherd, and when we see how he also exercises the functions of doctor and administrator. There is gentleness here but there is also firmness. This man who will so often be exercising mercy towards those under him must know that it is not always in the best interests of either individual or community to fail to reprove or to be unable to say enough is enough. Those who challenge his authority need to know how far they can go; without that there is no security, and growth into responsible maturity needs that security – as parents know. If I am too much of a permissive mother there is a point at which I may do my children an active dis-service by not taking a firm stand or giving them a framework to family life which asks of them that they observe certain limitations.

What St Benedict expects from his abbot, as from his monks, is obedience, listening to the Word, to the Rule, to the brothers. So from the first his power is curtailed, for no dictator can emerge from a person earthed in the demands made by true obedience. But more than this, the abbot reflects Christ whose place he holds, the Christ who throughout the Prologue was offering the 'way of life'. The love that he expresses is the love of Christ; the teaching that he is to deliver is the teaching of Christ himself. So what does it mean when the abbot is a teacher and the monastery a school? The best analogy is of a father teaching his children or a master his apprentices. The term 'school' as it is used in 'school of the Lord's service' is misleading if it carries any suggestion of formal education. Originally the word was used for a room or a hall in which people assembled for a common purpose, and in the Rule its usage means a group who have come together for the common purpose of seeking God. So it is both a place and a human group. But the learning process is more analogous to that of apprenticeship by which one person learns a skill from another. In the ancient world skills were handed down from father to son, and so apprenticeship also carries with it the implication of a father-son relationship. It involves imitation, and long, patient watching and copying, a shared learning that owes much to the fact of daily living together.

Then St Benedict introduces another subtle hint, showing a delicacy about education and learning that is far more sensitive than much that is practised in schools and colleges today. The abbot's guidance and teaching has to be introduced almost imperceptibly into the minds of the disciples, almost like leaven, so that they think they have taught it themselves (2.5). He uses an example which makes the point vividly to those who are today again making their own bread and thus familiar with that mysterious action of the yeast, first breaking into life itself and then animating that dull mass of flour until it is transformed and becomes something quite other, while still remaining in essence the same material.

This is not theoretical knowledge but practical knowledge of how to live, not formal and structured but given through personal contact, often in subtle ways. So the abbot's primary qualification is not intellectual or academic but 'goodness of life and wisdom in teaching' (64.2). He communicates by word and by deed, but even more by example; the message of his own life is more effective than what he says. St Benedict clearly thinks little of dry theological speculation and academic knowledge acquired through books, and in this, as so often, he reveals his firm grasp on reality. Ask anyone what really brought them to the Christian faith and enabled them to live and grow in it, and it is unlikely that they will say 'intellectual understanding'. It is more probable that their answer will be either some person whose way of life proved an inspiration, or that the practice of faith with all its demands of the lived life carried them along the way.

The abbot then is a man concerned to encourage his disciples to grow into their unique fullness as creatures of God and since no two are alike his daily nourishing, sustaining, correcting will be different in each case. In saying that he should 'love as he sees best for each individual' (6.14) the Rule coins a happy phrase. This is the good shepherd who knows each of his sheep and who adapts his loving care to the needs of each. St Benedict makes frequent use of the vocabulary of love, and it comes across nowhere more strongly than in the great image of the abbot as a good shepherd, the good shepherd of St John's gospel who cares for his sheep.

Caring is a word in such constant use – community care, a child in care – that it has become difficult to get back to its full meaning. It is a word much used in the second chapter in describing the role of the abbot, and it occurs elsewhere when the Rule discusses the abbot's care for the monk in trouble (27, 28). The image of the good shepherd brings this out, for it is the mark of the hireling to care nothing for the sheep while the good shepherd in contrast knows his own and his own know him, that reciprocal personal knowledge without which any complete caring is impossible. Caring involves healing, and the work of the abbot is also that of the physician, the skilful doctor. For St Benedict is setting up a caring community and when in his great chapter at the end, chapter 72, he concludes by laying down the supreme principle that what actually counts is love, he is giving a blueprint for any caring community. He knows that it is hard work, and that the brothers will have to labour hard at it. Nothing could be less vague or romantic than his treatment throughout the Rule of the way in which real love is to be fostered between members of the community, and that great panegyric at the end must not be taken out of the context of all the other places in which he talks about love in its most practical terms (as for example in the case of hospitality). The abbot, who is the exemplar of the qualities that all the brothers should have, must in the first place actually *be* good and loving rather than being able to talk about it, and he must show equal love to all. Only against this secure background of love can healing begin to take place, that life-long process which everyone needs. The abbot must know both how to heal his own wounds and those of others (46.6). In the first place he has to be skilled at diagnosing individual ills, so that he does not take the easy short cut of handing out the same cure to each. Instead the Rule is insistent that someone needs kindness, someone else needs severity, and while one will respond to reproof another will respond to persuasion.

It is never easy to live with other people; it is much simpler to be a saint alone. In a community, or a family, or a parish, or a group of friends, it is inevitable that we are going to be hurt time and again by others, sometimes so deeply that the pain retains its power for years afterwards. We wound each other so easily and so quickly. The Rule knows that these small cuts and bruises, these knocks and blows, the strange and hurtful things that we do to one another, can, if they are left untended, soon develop into running sores. That is why St Benedict orders the Lord's Prayer to be said twice a day so that 'forgive us our trespasses as we forgive those who trespass against us' will be a constant reminder of the vital necessity of practising forgiveness. To go round like Cain with hate of our brother leads to disaster. So the heart of community is forgiveness. We can only be healed through forgiveness, and we can only gain freedom through it. 'Forgiveness is the greatest factor of growth for any human being.' But it is demanding; it is an exercise which asks of us honesty and love. It brings us face to face with our pain, it forces us to confront it and deal with it, and St Benedict would add, the sooner the better, since unless they are cauterized wounds grow and fester. It is only too easy to keep up an internal conversation by which I chew over that hurting remark, or that undeserved happening, or I refuse to forget some slight, or I go on saying 'It isn't fair' over and over again to myself. Then what began as quite a small grudge or resentment has been nursed into a great brooding cloud that smothers all my inner landscape, or has become a cancer eating up more and more of my inner self. St Benedict is absolutely adamant about this. He describes it as murmuring or grumbling in the heart, and he is quite clear that it must be rooted out before it starts to do terrible damage. 'First and foremost, there must be no word or sign of the evil of grumbling, no manifestation of it for any reason at all' (34.6). For he knows that it is destructive of

133

peace of mind, both for the individual and the community. Peace is an overriding objective of Benedictine life, and *pax* has become a Benedictine watchword. 'Let peace be your request and aim' (Prol. 17); 'seek peace and pursue it.' Lack of interior peace threatens the whole fabric of the community and that is why St Benedict starts here, where that lack of peace begins, inside ourselves, with this murmuring which fragments and destroys us. When there is so much concern today with the peace of the world, when peace movements multiply and peace groups proliferate, and the discussion of peace-making becomes more and more urgent and insistent, St Benedict brings us back to this very simple and basic root: peace must start within myself. How can I hope to contribute to the peace of the world when I cannot resolve my own inner conflicts? When I am torn apart by my own internal stress? St Benedict is saying once again that I must take responsibility for myself, and that if I hope to achieve great things in the cause of peace I must start with peace at home, within myself. The chain of violence must end in me; this is the start of peace and where world peace must begin.

When things go wrong in the community and there is failure of one sort or another then this same readiness to take responsibility must not be evaded. After failure comes confession and then finally forgiveness. St Benedict chooses to illustrate this with the most practical of all occasions, damage in the storeroom. 'If someone commits a fault in the kitchen, in the storeroom, in serving, in the bakery, in the garden, in any craft or anywhere else – either by breaking or losing something or in any other way in any other place, he must at once come before the abbot and the community and of his own accord admit his fault and make satisfaction' (46. 1–4). In other words, he is insisting on owning up at once. What a childish phrase! And yet it means recognizing the real importance of taking responsibility for one's actions, being ready to say we are sorry, being willing to accept being forgiven. We know how utterly we can rely on God's acceptance and forgiveness of us, whoever we are and at whatever point in our life. 'Never to despair of the mercy of God' is one of the most important counsels of the Rule. The monk is no superman any more than we are. The ikon of the perfect monk is the publican repeating continually 'Lord I am a sinner' (Luke 18:13. 7.65). Sin is forgiven, and forgiveness is freely available to all who truly repent. And then with forgiveness comes that liberation which the present abbot of Mont de Cats reminds us, which 'because it comes from God, we will one day acknowledge as the only effective therapy for the distortions of our psyches and the aimless drift of our society.'

The way in which St Benedict deals with the question of failure and recovery by taking the example of trouble in the bakery and garden shows yet again how the Rule never sees the material and spiritual as though they are distinct and separate matters. We find this same perspective applies when St Benedict comes to present the adminstrative duties of the abbot. The good ordering of temporal affairs has always been a hallmark of the Benedictine life, and in practice it involves the abbot in a vast amount of organization. But St Benedict does not consider it as something on its own, set apart from the rest of life, for that would be quite contrary to all that he believes. The running of the institution is about people, its purpose is the formation of sons, and while he would no doubt approve the idea of business management today it would alarm him if its aims had ceased to reflect his holistic vision.

The role of the abbot then is not purely in the area of spiritual affairs; he is also responsible for the making of policy and for decisions about the temporal life of the community. Here is a high level of expectation, carrying the dangers of overwork, stress and tension, the hazards only too familiar to anyone in any form of top management today. St Benedict gives an exact description of a man under stress: excitable, anxious, overbearing, obstinate, jealous, over-suspicious and above all quite unable to stop, 'Such a man is never at rest' (64.16). Living at this sort of pressure not only makes impossible demands on oneself but carries the danger of imposing similar pressure on those around. 'If I drive my flocks too hard they will all die in a single day' (Genesis 33:13. 64.14), and therefore St Benedict insists on moderation and discretion, which he sees as quite fundamental virtues. The psychological insight which he brings to the whole area of business and administration shows a thoroughly sane grasp of human needs and capacities.

Delegation is an art. St Benedict recognizes the important role to be played by 'the kind of men with whom the abbot can confidently share the burdens of his office' (21.3), and the Rule makes provision for a whole range of officials who will share his burdens and relieve him of the care of certain groups within the community. In every case the men are chosen to fit the jobs; there is nothing automatic about seniority or status. Many are permanent appointments, others are to serve some more immediate purpose. St Benedict foresees that the abbot may well be the very last person whom a monk about to leave the monastery wants to see, and so at this most delicate moment he delegates his authority to men whose confidentiality he will respect, 'mature and wise brothers who, under the cloak of secrecy, may support the wavering brother' (27. 2–3). This argues confidence in his colleagues and offers a wise principle for others in positions of authority who might learn a lesson here: not only the immense significance of giving scope for an absolute confidentiality in dealings with colleagues, but also in accepting that often there is a proper moment in which to step down oneself and let another take over. Parents, for example, are likely to be the worst possible people to deal with adolescent rebellion. But the rejection of the father-figure ('the murder of the father') does not happen only in the family; it is something which has to be played out in many scenes later in life, and it calls for discretion and a willingness to share authority if it is to be dealt with creatively.

Building a successful community has a lot to do with keeping up morale. This does not happen without effort. St Benedict's ideas on this can be seen most clearly in the case of the cellarer, the man who in fact holds the job of bursar. He is an excellent example of what serving each other in love involves. The Rule cautions that he shall provide the brothers with their allotted amount of food 'without pride or delay' (31.16). St Benedict has here accurately observed one of the temptations of bureaucracy: to exercise power by making others feel small, even if by nothing more trivial than keeping them waiting. If he is not in a position to give what is asked for 'he will offer a kind word in reply', and when faced by an unreasonable demand from a brother he is still not to 'reject him with disdain and cause him distress' (31.7), but to refuse in a reasonable and humble way that will not sadden or upset him. Taking care to avoid unnecessary cause for hurt feelings sounds simple enough, but how wise St Benedict is to slip in a reminder about it. When I give a sharp response, or there is a curt note in my voice on the telephone and a brusque reply to a perfectly innocent enquiry, I could perfectly well stop for a moment and think of the distress that could mean to the other person, and it is really very little trouble to change my tone or soften my words. Sometimes of course the reason may be exhaustion, that I feel at the end of my tether because of the inroads that seem to be made upon my precious time. But here St Benedict brooks no excuses. It is up to the cellarer to keep regular and convenient hours, 'necessary items are to be requested and given at the proper time' (31.18). Being endlessly available to everyone does neither them nor myself any good in the end. If St Benedict tells the cellarer to protect himself that is a lesson I might well turn to my advantage. I find that the Rule is facing me again with the demands of self-love!

Others will respect my space if I take myself and my own demands seriously. And essentially this means that I work to keep my peace of mind and pay attention to my own morale;

animam suam custodiat is the Latin phrase of the Rule which I hold on to here. But how much more does anyone who is carrying a demanding role in any organization need to find a style of life which allows him or her to work with and for others and at the same time to retain sufficient resilience not to be drained by them. Using energy to the best possible advantage is a most urgent lesson for anyone in authority today, in business, in the parish, in any organization, as true now as it was for those exercising authority in the much less complex situation of St Benedict's day.

'Do everything with counsel and you will not be sorry afterwards' (Ecclesiasticus (Sirach) 32:24. 3.12) is a maxim which both safeguards the abbot from undue stress and the brothers from possible tyranny. The centrality of obedience is of course the key. Being obedient to all the brethren (as they in turn are obedient to each other) means listening to what they desire and advise, and so as a result there is nothing arbitrary or autocratic about the making of decisions. The abbot takes advice from all, irrespective of age or status. Yet the community is not to be run by majority votes. St Benedict also knows about the subtle pressures that can often be exerted by the weak and the frail, and the abbot is put on his guard against their demands, for there also is a definite tyranny that the weak and the unhappy can bring to bear in any community. Having listened to everyone, considered the Rule and any other way in which the Lord may speak, the abbot has then to sit down and reach his own decision in each particular instance. This is in fact discernment and sensitivity, trying to discover the will of God, the fruit of that wisdom which St Benedict looks for in the mature monk, and in the very different circumstances of decision-making today it still has much to offer.

It is noticeable how both the abbot and the cellarer are constantly concerned about the brethren, caring for each singly in all their uniqueness, rather than with the community *en bloc*, that ideal which seems to haunt so much contemporary ideology. The common life never becomes a piece of abstract idealization or idealism. St Benedict would probably have appreciated Dietrich Bonhoeffer's aphorism 'He who loves community destroys community; he who loves the brethren builds community'. So he begins with the brethren, with people as people, and there is for him no distinction of persons. There is however always consideration of needs. The Rule, in making distribution of goods according to needs, warns against the common pitfall that all should receive the same and instead asks for something which demands maturity and understanding on the part of the members of the community. 'We do not imply that there should be favouritism – God forbid! but rather consideration for weaknesses. Whoever needs less should thank God and not be distressed, but whoever needs more should feel humble because of his weakness, not self-important because of the kindness shown to him. In this way all the members will be at peace' (34. 2–5). Wanting fair shares is very natural and it is only as I grow in maturity, recognizing my own strengths and weaknesses and accepting those of others, that I begin to make any headway in what St Benedict is talking about here. Yet he knew this is essential in any community if there is to be that unity which St Paul envisages as the body of Christ, the whole which does not destroy the parts. For the quality of the common life can only be a reflection of the quality of the relationships between the individuals who make it up.

The Benedictine understanding of the common life is based on four underlying principles which show an extraordinarily humane understanding of how people best work together. First comes the principle of solidarity, which states that in every area of life, whether liturgical, social, economic, each member is equally concerned and responsible; there is no picking and choosing, no contracting out. Yet this is not blind conformity, for the next principle is that of pluralism, which recognizes the ultimate worth of every individual and so allows for the diversity of needs and gifts which grow from this. The principle of authority demands that the abbot, and those to whom he has delegated power, see that they exercise it without at the same time detracting from the final principle, that of subsidiarity. This means that what someone can manage to do themselves should not be entrusted to another in the name of 'higher authority'. So at the end there is a balance of inter-dependence and responsibility which allows the good of both the individual and the group to develop to their fullest.

THOUGHTS AND PRAYERS

Together we enjoyed sweet fellowship:
in the house of our God

(Psalm 55:15)

This, then, is the good zeal,
   which monks must foster with fervent love:
They should each try to be the first to show respect
                                    to the other
   supporting with the greatest patience
   one another's weaknesses of body or behaviour,
   and earnestly competing in obedience to one another.
No one is to pursue what he judges better for himself,
but instead, what he judges better for someone else.
   To their fellow monks they show the pure love
                                    of brothers;
   to God, loving fear;
   to their abbot, unfeigned and humble love.
Let them prefer nothing whatever to Christ,
and may he bring us all together to everlasting life.

(Rule of St Benedict 72, 3–12)

Why hast thou cast our lot
   In the same age and place,
And why together brought
   To see each other's face:
To join in loving sympathy,
And mix our friendly souls in thee?
Didst thou not make us one,
   That we might one remain,
Together travel on,
   And bear each other's pain;

141

Till all thy utmost goodness prove,
And rise renewed in perfect love?

(*Charles Wesley*)

He who dwells with brethren must not be square but round,
so as to turn himself to all.

(*Abba Matoes*)

There are two ways
    of bringing into communion
    the diversity of particular gifts:
        the love of sharing
        and the sharing of love.
Thus the particular gift becomes common
        to him who has it
        and to him who has it not:
            he who has it
                communicates it by sharing,
            he who has it not
                participates by communion.

(*Baldwin of Ford*)

One of the elders was asked what was humility, and he said:
If you forgive a brother who has injured you before he
himself asks pardon.

(*Desert Fathers: LXXXIV*)

Surrender your rights
    to another
surrender your rights
    to the other
whether friend or foe
    let them go
Christ is always
    the other.

God our Father, Lord of all the world,
we thank you that through your Son
you have called us into the fellowship
of your universal Church:
hear our prayer for your faithful people
that each in his vocation and ministry
may be an instrument of your love,
and give to your servants
the needful gifts of grace,
through our Lord and Saviour Jesus Christ.

NOTES

The patriarchal role of the abbot which is presented by Cuthbert Butler in his classical work *Benedictine Monachism*, Cambridge 1923, pp. 195ff is amplified by the commentary of the Collegeville text of the Rule, pp. 354. This chapter owes a lot to the section there 'The abbot as administrator', pp. 368–70.

The sentence I quote on page 133 on forgiveness is taken from an address given by Jean Vanier during a retreat in Canterbury cathedral in September 1983, 'Listening to God', and the quotation on page 135 from Dom André Louf 'Saint Benedict: A Man of God for all times', *Cistercian Studies*, 1980, XV, 3, pp. 217–29.

Two other articles which have helped me with this chapter are Marian Larmann *'Contristare* and *Tristitia* in the Rule of St Benedict: indications of community and morale', *American Benedictine Review*, June 1979, 30.2, pp. 159–74, and Mildred Murray-Sinclair, 'The Concept of Healing in the Rule of St Benedict', *Cistercian Studies*, 1980, XV, 3, pp. 269.

The concluding section of this chapter was taken almost entirely from Daniel Rees *Consider Your Call*, pp. 66–7.

But more than anything else this chapter has been inspired by a paper by Dom Bede Stockill, O.C.S.O. of Mount St Bernard Abbey, 'The Abbot in the Rule of St Benedict'.

The collect has been slightly adapted for the blessing of an abbot or abbess or the installation of the head of a community.

X

Praying

'everywhere in God's sight'

PRAYER LIES AT the very heart of the Benedictine life; it holds everything together, it sustains every other activity. It is at the same time root and fruit, foundation and fulfilment. The discussion of prayer comes at the end of this book but it might equally well have come at the beginning as the one thing that makes all the rest possible. For praying can never be set apart from the rest of life, it is the life itself. St Benedict did not ask his monks to take a vow to pray, for he expected prayer to be central in their lives, permeating whatever else they were doing. Prayer is *opus Dei*, the work of God, and nothing whatsoever is to be preferred to it. At least twice St Benedict says that nothing must be put before the love of Christ, and he uses precisely the same phrase 'to put nothing before' when he comes to talk of the divine office, as if that is the most excellent witness to the community's love of Christ, the pre-eminent occasion for the expression of that love.

St Benedict never loses sight of the primacy of love; the Rule might almost be called a handbook on the practice of loving. That living out of love in its most practical terms, which we struggle with every day, hinges on our love of Christ, the keystone of it all. And that, as St Benedict well knows, just as in human love, asks of us time and attention; just as in human love we can only come to love someone as we come to know them. That is why the Prologue told us that we had to stop and listen; that is why if prayer and love mean anything at all they mean entering into a dialogue

145

with God. The essential starting point for this must be that we on our part are ready to listen, open and attentive to the Word. 'The disciple is to be silent and listen' (6.6). How can you hear the Word until you are silent? 'Monks should diligently cultivate silence at all times' (42.1). When St Benedict devotes one chapter to the keeping of silence (in addition to the many references scattered throughout the Rule) it is about much more than not speaking. He is as concerned about the cessation of the inner noise as of the external chatter. After all, the foundation of his own life's work was the years of silence and solitude in the cave at Subiaco. The life of constant silence, let alone the life of a hermit, is certainly totally unthinkable for most of us, for whom even a few snatched moments of silence before the start of the day's work are often a luxury. Yet the underlying point about the essential value of silence is something which I cannot afford to disregard. Unless I am silent I shall not hear God, and until I hear him I shall not come to know him. Silence asks me to watch and wait and listen, to be like Mary in readiness to receive the Word. If I have any respect for God I shall try to find a time, however short, for silence. Without it I have not much hope of establishing that relationship with God of hearing and responding which is going to help me root the whole of my life in prayer.

St Benedict has been quite clear, ever since he greeted us in the Prologue with his challenge, that the Word of God demands our response. The Rule has shown that this is not a challenge once and for all; rather, since the Word is heard daily it presents the monk with a daily encounter with God. He hears him in the liturgy and the psalms, in public reading at meals and in his private reading, study and meditation. The pattern of his day is marked by alternative listening and answering, sometimes in a corporate setting, sometimes in a personal one. A very high proportion of his time is thus given over to reading and reflecting on the Scriptures. More or less four hours a day are assigned to *lectio divina,* prayerful private reading and *meditatio,* the memorization, repetition and reflection of biblical texts. On Sundays reading takes the place of manual labour, and there is time for extra reading in Lent, the season in which St Benedict is looking for special growth in the spiritual life. He gives a severe warning about any monk who wastes time 'to the neglect of his reading and so not only harms himself but also distracts others. If such a monk is found – God forbid – he should be reproved a first and a second time. If he does not amend he must be subjected to the punishment of the Rule as a warning to others' (48. 18–20). In the saying of the daily offices, which occupy another four hours or so of the day, the monk will also hear the Word, and will listen, this time in the company of the brethren, to the story of God's dealing with his people, and will join with them in singing the psalms. At the hour of the divine office anything else in the monastery must be immediately abandoned: the work of God takes precedence. So the Rule ensures that every day is marked by frequent, regular times at which the monk hears the Word of God.

For St Benedict, so totally formed in the mentality of the Bible himself, wants the same for his monks. His belief in the power of the Scriptures is seen in the images he uses in speaking of them. The Gospel is our guide (Prol. 21); medicine (28.3); divine law (53.9); the rock on which to build (Prol. 33); the treasury on which to draw (64.9). These images make the point that reading is not to stop short at the acquisition of mere knowledge, above all it should form the basis of a continuing dialogue with Christ which will colour the actual quality and experience of daily living. All this is so far removed from the art of reading as I practise it today that it is only by a very considerable effort of the imagination that I can recapture the full sense of what it would have involved in St Benedict's day. Reading is now for most of the time such a basic fact of existence that I take it entirely for granted, whether it means following the instructions on the back of a packet, or glancing at the times of television programmes in the paper, or keeping up with the latest novel of my favourite author. If I am reading something which is ephemeral I pay scant attention to it, and if I am reading more serious material I then apply my critical faculties and assess it with a detached, intellectual approach. But St Benedict assumes that the whole of the body, and thus the whole of the person, is engaged in the act of reading. Words are tasted to release their full flavour, weighed in order to sound the full depths of their meaning. It is not only that it was customary to pronounce the words with the lips in a low tone so that they were heard as well as seen, they were also learnt 'by heart' in the fullest sense of that phrase, which again we have lost, but which means with the whole being. So the Scriptures are mouthed by the lips, understood by the intelligence, fixed by the memory, and finally the will comes into play and what has been read is also put into practice. The act of reading makes the reader become a different person; reading cannot be separated from living.

The very first thing that is asked of the novice at the solemn moment of his profession, after signing the vows and laying them on the altar, is that he begin a verse from the psalms. '*Suscipe me*, uphold me, O Lord, as you have promised and I shall live; do not disappoint me in my hope' (Psalm 118(119): 116. 58.21). The psalms are there to speak to every occasion and every need, and St Benedict gives them a central place in the prayer life of the monastery. He is himself so soaked in their thought and language that the Rule contains more quotations from the psalms than from the New Testament. He looks for the same familiarity from his disciples. The number of psalms is never reduced even though at certain times of the year other readings might have to be shortened (10). If the entire psalter is covered each week then indeed the monk must come to have the psalms written on his heart, engraved in his memory.

In his concern that his monks should know and love the psalms St Benedict showed himself a shrewd judge of human needs, for here is a book which plumbs the depths as well as the heights for all of us. In the psalms I find myself at my worst and my best. Here I can acclaim God with warmth and confidence and hope, but here also I can give vent to those black thoughts that might otherwise lie hidden in the dark and angry corners of my heart. Above all the psalms express the reality of my longing for God and my joy and sufferings in the vicissitude of my search for him. Sometimes God is close, sometimes distant. I seek him in the desert and on the mountain, in poverty and in emptiness and in waiting. Today God is mindful of me, tomorrow he may not visit me. Today I am brought to the mountain top, tomorrow I am calling from the depths. Today I am radiant, tomorrow I face darkness. Today I enjoy life, tomorrow I feel the hand of death.

Although he wants his monks to pray without ceasing, as we know from his own life St Benedict did himself, he knows that spontaneity must be upheld by structure and freedom by ritual; that the personal prayer also needs corporate prayer and that the awareness of the presence of God needs to be fed from time to time from sources external to oneself. So he imposes a rhythm and form on the life of prayer, as he does on other aspects of the monastic life, since it is part of his wisdom to recognize the need for balance in each day, each week, and each year. He has a great deal to say about the organization of the seven daily offices; in fact eleven chapters are devoted to extremely careful notes about the performance of the liturgy. Yet he opens with no formal treatise on the theology of worship, no principles on the art of prayer or analysis of the state of mind and attitude of the soul before its creator. On the contrary, he plunges starkly into the most practical details possible about the saying of the night office. 'By sleeping until a little past the middle of the night the brothers can arise with their food fully digested . . . the time for Vigils should be adjusted so that a very short interval after Vigils will give the monks opportunity to care for nature's needs' (8. 2,4). Instead of theory (and that is something we are not short of since spirituality has become one of the most popular genres of religious writing) St Benedict seems to be telling us simply to get on with the business of praying, and not to neglect the very proper demands of the body while we are doing it. The thought that my prayer will not be any less profitable if I do not suffer physical discomfort is a consoling message in the face of a lingering Puritan assumption that somehow suffering must always be good for the soul . . . If I can sit to pray, or lie down, and be at ease with myself without feeling guilty, that is good to hold on to – and it will not make my prayer any the less effective because I am taking my body seriously.

The saying of the offices seven times so that each stage of the day's work may be appropriately offered to God is humanly speaking far beyond anything those of us outside the monastic life could hope to follow. Although the Rule was written with the agricultural life of the sixth century in mind, the underlying principle of the hallowing of time and work still deserves consideration in terms which make sense for the twentieth century. How can we offer the pattern of the day to God as we answer the relentless demands of our complex timetables? Certainly for St Benedict it was a matter of the utmost importance. 'On hearing the signal for an hour of the divine office, the monk will immediately set aside what he has in hand and go with the utmost speed, yet with gravity and without giving occasion for frivolity. Indeed, nothing is to be preferred to the work of God' (43. 1–3). This is of course a corporate activity and before I go on to see how I can make the daily offices into something applicable to myself at home or at work it is important that I do not lose sight of the role that St Benedict assigns to praying together and to sharing worship. Just because prayer is so personal and arises from the centre of my being it might develop into some individualistic self-indulgence unless anchored in the local community to which I belong. My praying must not become so hidden and so secret that it becomes an entirely private affair, no longer supported by others and by the mutual learning which contact with other people brings.

In chapter 16, in summing up the purpose of the daily office, St Benedict uses the word 'praise' five times in as many sentences. He is quoting, as so often, from the psalms. 'Seven times a day have I praised you' (Psalm 118 (119); 164. 16.1). Alleluia, or 'We praise you, God' or 'Glory be to the Father', all refrains which litter the saying of the offices may be the clue that shows the way in which I might adapt what they are doing to the very different scene of my own daily situation. Perhaps even more illuminating are the practical examples which St Benedict gives of the times outside those times of formal prayer at which the monk offers that particular happening, that particular person, to God with a brief prayer. The start of routine duties, the beginning and ending of meals, the welcoming of a guest, all these are occasions for short prayer. The weekly reader asks all to pray for him; so does the weekly server; so does the monk setting out on a journey. The porter responds to a knock with 'God bless you' or 'Thanks be to God!' This is a re-focusing of our attention on God at specific moments. If we care to translate this into our own terms grace before meals is likely to be the only obvious occasion we have in common with the life described by the Rule. Yet many cultures since St Benedict's day have found it possible to integrate prayer and daily life totally unselfconsciously, and I think we have much to learn from this. In the Outer Hebrides, for example, men and women managed to bring to every occasion of their daily lives a prayer or poem in which to celebrate God, whatever the time of day and whatever the task that might be engaging them. Getting up and washing, lighting the fire and milking the cow, driving the flocks and making butter, are all offered up in prayer. It is undoubtedly much less romantic (though if I am honest, also less gruelling) to put on the kettle, to get out the car, to deal with the morning's post, and so on throughout the day. But that is no reason for not trying to make each of these an occasion for prayer, not necessarily self-consciously in words (though a prayer like 'Thanks be to God' may come easily to mind) but much more simply by attending to the moment, to what it means, and to how it can be seen as God-given. Often this is little more than heightening awareness, not taking for granted, the paying of full attention to what I am doing. I can switch on my electric kettle automatically, or I can stop and thank God for those unseen people responsible for bringing that electric current into my house. Instead of fuming and cursing at the maddening driver of the car in front of me I can use his erratic and uncertain driving to prompt me to make intercession for someone who possibly stands in particular need of God's loving care at that moment. Shopping, my least favourite occupation, presents me with endless opportunities to find God in otherwise trying people and situations. For even when I may pray in words, in the last resort the words are not important, not actually necessary at all. The heart of it is my total attentiveness to God. This is an amazing, liberating realization and of course this needs constant recalling and constant practice; yet I do find that whenever I remember it makes a great difference to the quality and enjoyment of each day. For really the Rule is telling me that ultimately praying is living, working, loving, accepting, the refusal to take anything or anyone for granted but rather to try to find Christ in and through them all.

'We believe that the divine presence is everywhere and that in every place the eyes of the Lord are watching' (Proverbs 15:3. 19.1). This sense of the constant presence of God is something which St Benedict is anxious that we should never forget. God's gaze is fixed on us, our thoughts and actions lie totally open to his view, we are always seen, everywhere in God's sight (7.10–13). Our awareness of God's presence must be the ever immediate reality which underpins everything else. How amazingly uncomplicated St Benedict makes the way to God. It is totally demanding but it is not out of reach.

What St Benedict is really looking for then is that continual prayer which goes on all the time; it is the *always* of that line of the psalms which he uses in chapter seven. 'That a man keeps the fear of God always before his eyes' (Psalm 35(36):2. 7.10). Here we have moved beyond words. This is total attentiveness to the presence of God. It is the fruit of the whole and balanced person which the Benedictine life has been trying to foster, and of the sense of the all-embracing presence of Christ which runs throughout the Rule. For Christ *is* to be found in the circumstances, the people, the things of daily life. St Benedict hopes that if we are continually aware of this we shall lift our hearts to him and in this way our whole life will become prayer in action. So here we see that the final purpose of the monastic life is not the *opus Dei,* the work of God as it is celebrated in the divine office, but the work of God in uninterrupted prayer, which is the search for God in all things. And this is not so difficult if it is not merely confined to the mind but engages the whole being, will, emotions, senses, body, intelligence, all that goes to make up each of us as we are, separately and individually. So prayer is not in competition with other activities, and growth in prayer will not be encouraged by the withdrawal from other work if our intention is that every action should be directed towards God. We pray from the same base as we live. Our prayer reflects the way in which we respond to life itself, and so our prayer can only be as good as the way we live. God will not be taken in by fine words any more than the shrewd St Benedict will be taken in by the monk whose mind is not in harmony with his voice as he sings the psalms. The whole Christ is seeking the whole person.

All this would of course be impossible if the initiative and the activity lay with us. Mercifully that is not the case. While we are seeking God he is also seeking us. The work of God has two senses: our offering to God and his work in us. This asks of us not so much that we actually say prayers as that we live open to grace. If we do use words they will be

153

those of the publican, standing there with open hands, waiting, confessing his utter reliance upon God. Perhaps the best way of describing St Benedict's way of prayer is to say that it is the natural outcome of a life dedicated to grace. He treats the subject with modesty and with brevity, and yet the whole content of the Benedictine life emanates from prayer, understood in its broadest context as relationship with God; a life lived in his presence in a growing, permeating consciousness of what that presence means. St Benedict is giving us the chance to stand where, if we are truly seeking God, we know that we shall be found by him.

THOUGHTS AND PRAYERS

Nevertheless I am always with you:
for you hold me by my right hand

(Psalm 73:23)

... being attentive to the times of the day: when the birds began to sing, and the deer came out of the morning fog, and the sun came up. The reason why we don't take time is a feeling that we have to keep moving. This is a real sickness. We live in the fullness of time. Every moment is God's own good time, His kairos. The whole thing boils down to giving ourselves in prayer a chance to realize that we have what we seek. We don't have to rush after it. It was there all the time, and if we give it time, it will make itself known to us.

(Thomas Merton)

One act is required – and that is all: for this one act pulls everything together and keeps everything in order. . . . This one act is to stand with attention in your heart.

(Theophan the Recluse)

My walk this day with God,
My walk this day with Christ,
My walk this day with Spirit,
   The Three-fold all-kindly:
   Ho! ho! ho! the Three-fold all-kindly.

My shielding this day from ill,
My shielding this night from harm,
Ho! ho! both my soul and my body,
   By Father, by Son, by Holy Spirit,
   By Father, by Son, by Holy Spirit.

Be the Father shielding me,
Be the Son shielding me,
Be the Spirit shielding me,
    As Three and as One:
    Ho! ho! ho! as Three and as One.

(Celtic journeying song)

God gives prayer to the man who prays

(John Climacus)

Begin then to praise now, if thou intendest to praise for
ever ... Praise and bless the Lord thy God every single day,
so that when the time of single days has passed, and there
has come that one day without end, thou mayest go from
praise to praise, as 'from strength to strength'.

(St Augustine)

I looked
at him, not with the eye
only, but with the whole
of my being, overflowing with
him as a chalice would
with the sea.

(R. S. Thomas)

I think, Lord, that what you give me and everyone in prayer
is a new vision, or a new dimension. The people I am fond of
and love, the things I like doing, the places I like, are in
some tangible way different, added to, increased by you ...
The people and places and activities which I love and like
become different in you ... Lord, I may be being heretical or
untheological, but I don't mind and you know what I mean,
when I say that your abiding presence – yes, that's it Lord,
prayer is your abiding presence made real.

(Dom Dominic Gaisford)

Almighty and everlasting God,
who art always more ready to hear than we to pray,
and art wont to give more than either we desire, or deserve;
pour down upon us the abundance of thy mercy;
forgiving us those things
whereof our conscience is afraid,
and giving us those good things
which we are not worthy to ask,
but through the merits and mediation
of Jesus Christ, the Son, our Lord.

NOTES

This is a very largely personal interpretation but it has been influenced by two articles for which I am grateful. Michael Casey, 'St Benedict's approach to prayer', *Cistercian Studies*, 1980, XV, pp. 327–43, and David Holly, 'Biblical Living', *Cistercian Studies*, 1975, X, pp. 46–60.

The classical account of *lectio divina* is that of Dom Jean LeClerq, *The Love of Learning and the Desire for God. A Study of Monastic Culture*, SPCK, 1974.

I find that I have returned again to the Celtic prayers that I have used before, the *Carmina Gadelica* (see the notes at the end of chapter VI). Ever since I first discovered them they seemed to give me something for which I was searching: the possibility of contemplation in the midst of busyness (though I feel sure they would find this a self-conscious way of expressing it!) and of turning the actual activity itself into a way of praying continually.

In 'Thoughts and Prayers' the Thomas Merton quotation comes from *A Hidden Wholeness*, p. 49.

The Celtic journeying song from *Carmina Gadelica*, III, 48–9 is one of many I might have chosen, but I decided on this one because it shows that men and women can actually laugh as they walk every day with God, and this is something I feel we don't do nearly often enough.

The verse of R. S. Thomas is taken from 'Suddenly', *Laboratories of the Spirit*, Macmillan, 1975, p. 32.

Dom Dominic Gaisford's reflections on prayer come in his chapter 'Cast your bread on the waters,' in *A Touch of God*, p. 79.

The collect is for Trinity XII.

Notes on Further Reading

The classical account of the Rule remains that by Dom Cuthbert Butler, *Benedictine Monachism*, Cambridge, 1923, 2nd ed. 1961.

For those who might be happier with something a little shorter I think that Dom David Knowles *The Benedictines,* Sheed and Ward, 1929 is admirably clear and lucid.

The most illuminating modern study (and one to which this book is deeply indebted) is that edited by Daniel Rees and others, *Consider Your Call. A Theology of the Monastic Life Today,* SPCK, 1978, which has profoundly important things to say to our contemporary situation.

Dom David Parry O.S.B., in *Households of God*, Darton, Longman & Todd, 1980 sets out the Rule chapter by chapter, with expositions and explanations for monks and lay people today.

In 'Letter and Spirit: St Benedict's Rule Today', *The Way*, Supplement 40, Spring 1981, pp. 14–64, Dom Columba Cary-Elwes, O.S.B., gives one of the best possible introductions to the Rule.

The present Archbishop of Westminster, Cardinal Basil Hume, O.S.B., has published his devotional addresses to the monks of Ampleforth on monastic life and work, *Searching for God,* Hodder & Stoughton, 1977, re-issued in an illustrated edition 1979. See also his *In Praise of Benedict*, Hodder & Stoughton, 1980, sermons and talks on the Benedictine tradition given in the year which celebrated 1500 years of the Rule.

In *The Ordinary Way, A Family Spirituality*, Crossroad, New York, 1982, Dolores Leckey explores the way in which the Rule can illuminate family life – something which I also looked at in a short chapter, 'The Benedictine Tradition and the Family', *Journey to God, Anglican Essays on the Benedictine Way*, Malling Abbey, 1980.

The Benedictines in Britain, British Library series No. 3, 1980, is a clear, short historical survey, beautifully illustrated.

For a more comprehensive, yet brief, survey of the history of monasticism in general I think the best account is that of David Knowles, *Christian Monasticism*, World University Library, 1969.

Finally, the best insight into the Benedictine life today comes from *A Touch of God, Eight Monastic Journeys*, edited by Maria Boulding, SPCK, 1982, in which eight present-day members of the Benedictine Order, men and women, tell quite simply what that life means to them and the part that the Rule plays in their journey to God. This is a book which shows that the monastic life can illuminate the way for all Christians.